Grazing and Growing

American Society of Missiology
Monograph Series

Series Editor, James R. Krabill

The ASM Monograph Series provides a forum for publishing quality dissertations and studies in the field of missiology. Collaborating with Pickwick Publications—a division of Wipf and Stock Publishers of Eugene, Oregon—the American Society of Missiology selects high quality dissertations and other monographic studies that offer research materials in mission studies for scholars, mission and church leaders, and the academic community at large. The ASM seeks scholarly work for publication in the series that throws light on issues confronting Christian world mission in its cultural, social, historical, biblical, and theological dimensions.

Missiology is an academic field that brings together scholars whose professional training ranges from doctoral-level preparation in areas such as Scripture, history and sociology of religions, anthropology, theology, international relations, interreligious interchange, mission history, inculturation, and church law. The American Society of Missiology, which sponsors this series, is an ecumenical body drawing members from Independent and Ecumenical Protestant, Catholic, Orthodox, and other traditions. Members of the ASM are united by their commitment to reflect on and do scholarly work relating to both mission history and the present-day mission of the church. The ASM Monograph Series aims to publish works of exceptional merit on specialized topics, with particular attention given to work by younger scholars, the dissemination and publication of which is difficult under the economic pressures of standard publishing models.

Persons seeking information about the ASM or the guidelines for having their dissertations considered for publication in the ASM Monograph Series should consult the Society's website—www.asmweb.org.

Members of the ASM Monograph Committe who approved this book are:

   Robert Gallagher, Associate Professor of Intercultural Studies
           and Director of M.A. (Intercultural Studies),
               Wheaton College

   Margaret Guider, O.S.F., Associate Professor of Missiology, Boston College

Recently Published in the ASM Monograph Series

Clive S. Chin, *The Perception of Christianity as a Rational Religion in Singapore: A Missiological Analysis of Christian Conversion*

Matthew Friedman, *Union with God in Christ: Early Christian and Wesleyan Spirituality as an Approach to Islamic Mysticism*

Grazing and Growing

*Developing Disciples through
Contextualized Worship Arts in Mozambique*

By Megan Meyers

American Society of Missiology Monograph
Series vol. 33

☙PICKWICK *Publications* · Eugene, Oregon

GRAZING AND GROWING
Developing Disciples through Contextualized Worship Arts in Mozambique

American Society of Missiology Monograph Series 33

Copyright © 2018 Megan Meyers. All rights reserved. Except for brief quotations in critical publications or reviews, no part of this book may be reproduced in any manner without prior written permission from the publisher. Write: Permissions, Wipf and Stock Publishers, 199 W. 8th Ave., Suite 3, Eugene, OR 97401.

Pickwick Publications
An Imprint of Wipf and Stock Publishers
199 W. 8th Ave., Suite 3
Eugene, OR 97401

www.wipfandstock.com

PAPERBACK ISBN: 978-1-5326-1961-8
HARDCOVER ISBN: 978-1-4982-4601-9
EBOOK ISBN: 978-1-4982-4600-2

Cataloguing-in-Publication data:

Names: Meyers, Megan.

Title: Grazing and growing : developing disciples through contextualized worship arts in Mozambique / by Megan Meyers.

Description: Eugene, OR: Pickwick Publications, 2018 | American Society of Missiology Monograph Series 33 | Includes bibliographical references.

Identifiers: ISBN 978-1-5326-1961-8 (paperback) | ISBN 978-1-4982-4601-9 (hardcover) | ISBN 978-1-4982-4600-2 (ebook)

Subjects: LCSH: Public worship. | Music—Religious aspects. | Christianity—Mozambique. | Ethnomusicology.

Classification: LCC ML3760 M35 2018 (print) | LCC ML3760 (ebook)

Scriptures taken from the Holy Bible, New International Version®, NIV®. Copyright © 1973, 1978, 1984, 2011 by Biblica, Inc.™ Used by permission of Zondervan. All rights reserved worldwide. www.zondervan.com. The "NIV" and "New International Version" are trademarks registered in the United States Patent and Trademark Office by Biblica, Inc.™

Permission granted by Baylor University Press to reuse the figure "A Matrix for Studies in Global Church Music (Studies in Ethnomusicology and the Christian Faith)," *Music in the Life of the African Church* (King 2008) with modifications.

Parts of this publication originally appeared in *Evangelical Missions Quarterly* (July 2016), and *Missiology: An International Review*, vol 44, no 3, July 2016. Permission to re-print has been graciously given.

Manufactured in the U.S.A. 02/23/18

To God be the glory, great things He has done!

To Brian Knickerbocker Meyers, my faithful and loving husband, who patiently endured and encouraged me "not to become weary in well doing." May we together "reap a harvest of blessing!"

To my four beautiful daughters, Jordan Marie, Eden Joy, Zion Grace, and Kidron Mae Faith, who "shine like stars" for God. May you continue to grow "in wisdom, in stature, and in favor with God and men."

To my dear Mozambican brothers and sisters in Christ who honor me with their wisdom and bless me with their music. May we continue to rehearse today for our worship together around the throne of the Lamb.

"The goat must graze where it is tied."
(Joaquim Alberto Chissano, first elected president of Mozambique)

Contents

List of Tables | ix
List of Figures | x
Acknowledgments | xiii
Abbreviations | xv

Introduction: The Goat Must Graze Where It Is Tied | 1

PART ONE: THE LANDSCAPE: EXPLORING MOZAMBICAN MUSIC-CULTURE VALUES | 9

1. Mozambique's Musical Context: Multicultural Migration and Missions | 11
2. The Literary Lay of the Land | 19
3. Forming the Fence: Research Design and Method Review | 36

PART TWO: THE PASTURE: DISCOVERING PRESENT STATE OF CHURCH CONTEXTS | 49

4. Gathering the Goats: What Does Worship Look Like in Beira? | 51
5. Vetting the Herd: Data Analysis | 69

PART THREE: GRAZING AND GROWING: ADAPTIVE CHANGE THROUGH WORSHIP PRAXIS | 85

6 Songwriting Workshop Method Expanded and Applied | 87
7 Results Assessment: What Happened? | 103

Conclusion: Grazing, Growing, and Going | 121

Appendix A: Research Schedule | 133
Appendix B: Case Summaries | 136
Appendix C: Sample Event Observation Report | 152
Appendix D: Field Notes Quoted | 158
Appendix E: Structured Interview Compiled Responses | 160
Appendix F: Lyric Theology | 163
Appendix G: Questionnaire Data | 168
Appendix H: Follow-Up Structured Interview Compiled Responses | 174

Vita | 176

References Cited | 179

Tables

Table 1: Comparison of Religions in Mozambique | 17
Table 2: Beira Church Demographics | 54
Table 3: Sample Content Analysis Form | 78
Table 4: Names for God | 79
Table 5: Song Subjects, Themes, and Frequency | 79
Table 6: Song Functions | 81
Table 7: Focus Group Interviews Timetable | 91
Table 8: Composer's Clubs Demographics | 98
Table 9: Church Participation in Research Phases | 117

Figures

Figure 1: Aerial View of Beira | 13
Figures 2a and 2b: Sena and Ndau Language Maps | 14
Figure 3: Elements of a Music Performance | 57
Figure 4: Church Layout | 58
Figure 5: Sanctuary | 59
Figure 6: Offering | 62
Figure 7: Songs Analyzed | 65
Figure 8: Processional | 67
Figure 9: Themes per Song Style | 80
Figure 10: Participation in Change Process Activities | 107
Figure 11: Impact of Change Process Activities | 109
Figure 12: Beira Gospel Concert | 111
Figure 13: Four-Arena Approach to Ethnomusicology-in-Mission | 122
Figure 14: Missiological Implications of Contextual Worship Arts | 123
Figure 15: Pastor João Salvador Sitoe | 136
Figure 16: Pastor Jeito Mandongue José (and wife, Marta) | 137
Figure 17: Pastor Agustinho José Xavier (Lázaro) | 139
Figure 18: Pastor Manuel Pequenino (on right) with co-workers | 140
Figure 19: Youth President Teófilo | 141
Figure 20: Pastor Luis Jofessa Nyazeze | 142

Figure 21: Pastor Mafucha Madoda Mateus | 143
Figure 22: Pastor Alexandre João Maunze | 144
Figure 23: Pastors Manuel Moises Quembo and
    Arão Simone Mbulu | 145
Figure 24: Pastor Tomás Pereira Viageiro | 146
Figure 25: Pastor Feliciano Adriano Cohauela | 147
Figure 26: Pastor Anacleto Luis Ferrão | 148
Figure 27: Pastor José Francisco Madeira | 150
Figure 28: Map of Vila Massane (ADI) | 152
Figure 29: Admired Church Qualities | 162

Acknowledgments

How does one describe an ocean? Words cannot adequately express the multitude of individual drops that contribute to the collective whole of the sea. Yet, it was a host of people who diligently and patiently worked with me to create this assemblage of words, and it is my great pleasure to attempt to account for each one that helped along the way.

First and foremost, I want to acknowledge my Creator, who, as the Master Craftsman, made a way for me to begin and to complete this book. He deserves all the honor and glory.

I need to thank my family, Brian, Jordan, Eden, Zion, and Kidron, for being flexible and patient, allowing "mommy" to be busy with the things of God outside of the home. I also want to thank the incredible people who graciously "stood in the gap" while I was being a student, including but not limited to Claude and Marilynn Meyers, Chumley and Connie Eckerle, Lydia Donoghue, Kate Cramer-Herbst, Anne-Marie Buijs-den Ouden, ShaCha Nalls, Galdina Neves Madeira, Fatima Vidigal, Minés José Manuel ("Pali"), Miquitaio Torres Miquitaio, and Valentim Pedro Mututua.

I also want to convey my appreciation to WorldVenture, particularly my Mozambique team colleagues Rob and Heather Blanks, Rodger and Lynn Schmidt, and Dave and Amy Terpstra, and the Africa Field Directors Glenn and Kathy Kendall, and Lloyd and Jan Chin, for cheering me on each step of the way.

I would also like to express my deep gratitude for the vast team of people who helped me along this research journey. First of all, the research partners who tirelessly worked to clarify and correct me, and to continue the work in my absence, Manuel Mário Armando, Pastor João Salvador Sitoe, and Djongue Juma. Second, the research assistants Bernardo Guacha and Quizito Manaene, who meticulously conducted content analysis with me.

Third, I express my deep gratitude to the pastors who generously allowed me access to their hearts and to their churches for this research, João Salvador Sitoe (VFC), Arão Simone Mbulu and Manuel Moises Quembo (1stB), Jeito Mandongue José (VPD), Manuel Pequenino (UB), Luis Jofesse Nyazeze (NA), Mafucha Madoda Mateus and Antonio Mucavare Zinharime (ECD), Agustinho José Xavier (ADI), Alexandre João Maunze (ADE), Anacleto Luis Ferrão (ADA), Tomás Pereira Viageiro (MEVN), Feliciano Adriano Cohauela (AM), and José Francisco Madeira (AB). Fourth, the numerous musicians and worship leaders in Beira who have offered me fellowship and friendship and inspired me to begin this research.

I would also like to thank my readers who painstakingly combed through the fine details of this paper and helped me create a clear and compelling dissertation, Lynne Boese, Karis Koehn, Tim and Beth Wood, Helder Andrade, and Manuel Mário; as well as my sub-cohort peers (the "ethno-femmes") who waded through the numerous permutations of this study throughout the course of three years, Lila Balisky, Amelia Koh-Butler, and Sue Whittaker.

Last (but not least), I want to thank my dear professor, mentor, friend, and role model Roberta R. King, who for some reason decided to put up with me once again for another degree at Fuller. You have taught me how to sing His praises in my heart and around the world, and for that I am eternally grateful. I cannot wait to sit next to you in the celestial choir!

Abbreviations

AB American Board (United Church of Christ)
ADA Assembleia de Deus Africana (African Assemblies of God)
ADE Assembleia de Deus Evangêlica (Evangelical Assemblies of God)
ADI Assembleia de Deus Internacional (International Assemblies of God)
AICs African-Initiated Churches
AIM Africa Inland Mission
AM Aurora Messiânica (Messianic Aurora)
ATRs African Traditional Religions
1stB Primeira Igreja Baptista (First Baptist Church)
ECD Evangelho Completo de Deus (Full Gospel Church of God)
FRELIMO Frente de Libertação de Moçambique (Mozambique Liberation Front)
IBS Instituto Bíblico de Sofala (Sofala Bible Institute)
MEVN Missão Evangêlica Vida Nova (Evangelical Mission of New Life)
NA Nova Aliança (New Alliance)
PAR Participatory Action Research

Abbreviations

PIDE	Polícia Internacional e de Defesa do Estado (Portuguese Secret Service)
UB	União Baptista (United Baptist)
VFC	Família Vitoriosa (Victory Family Center)
VPD	Visão na Palavra de Deus (Vision in the Word of God)
WICs	Western-Initiated Churches

INTRODUCTION

The Goat Must Graze Where It Is Tied

"Why don't you share some Christian songs in your language with me?" I asked a group of young Mozambican worship leaders. We were on our way home from a worship event in which we had sung familiar Western worship songs[1] translated into Portuguese. I had noticed that the participants (a group of youth with varied religious backgrounds, ranging from evangelical to nominal Catholic to Muslim) politely participated, but it somehow seemed a bit flat. As an ethnodoxologist,[2] I thought that perhaps the lack of enthusiasm during the event was due to the use of foreign songs. I naively assumed my friends would be thrilled to sing in their heart language.

Imagine my surprise when, with some embarrassment, they mumbled two short songs in Ndau.[3] It was far less than the enthusiastic response I had anticipated. Upon pressing for more detail as to their hesitancy, they responded simply, "That music has no life!"[4] It was clear that neither the foreign songs nor the indigenous hymnody currently in use were effective means of discipleship.

---

1. "Let it Rain," and "Open the Eyes of my Heart, Lord" (to name a few).

2. Ethnodoxology, first coined by David Hall, is "an application of ethnomusicology, ethnic arts studies, worship studies, missiology, and related disciplines. Those in this field study local musical traditions and work with local musicians and churches to adapt and develop locally created musical forms for Christian worship" (see "Ethnodoxology," Wikipedia, http://en.wikipedia.org/wiki/Ethnodoxology).

3. Ndau and Sena are the two major languages spoken in Beira, Mozambique.

4. See Appendix D for complete list of field notes referenced throughout study.

Joaquim Alberto Chissano, the first elected president of Mozambique, made famous the proverb, "The goat must graze where it is tied." Though he was responding to questions of governmental corruption, the principle holds true in church ministry and mission. Believers (goats) should be able to graze in the church where they are tied. One of the primary ways Christians are fed is through worship, for it is in worship where we encounter God and are transformed. These musicians' response to my questions convinced me of the necessity of developing a functional model of indigenous hymnody and contextualized worship arts within the local church, helping believers graze and grow in their faith through song.

BACKGROUND

Mozambique is a country whose evangelical Protestant missionary influence has a short history,[5] and whose Catholic presence has been plagued by its historical connection to Portuguese colonial ambitions. This translates into a Mozambican church that is, at large, young (both in terms of age and experience), minimally educated, and under-resourced. It is still quite malleable and open to growth and development through education and experience.

The goal of missions, and indeed the local church, is to develop disciples, people who worship and serve God wholeheartedly. John Piper states, "Worship . . . is the fuel and goal in missions."[6] Worship arts, then, can play a key role in church growth and development, through evangelism, leadership training, and discipleship, yet they are underutilized in ministry and missions.

With some notable exceptions, the practice of contextualized worship arts is not common in the city of Beira.[7] Many songs sung in churches are imported (primarily from Brazil or Australia) rather than

---

5. Evangelicals were late-comers to the mission field of Mozambique, not arriving until the late nineteenth century in the southern and central regions of the country (Chamango, *Chegada*, 7, 15). According to Chamango, before the Berlin conference in 1885 the Protestant churches and missionary societies were not officially allowed to operate in Mozambique, but after this historic conference Protestants gained relative freedom to work in the country. By the 1930s there were about eighteen Protestant missions operating throughout the country—some proselytizing from neighboring South Africa or Zimbabwe.

6. Piper, *Let the Nations be Glad*, 11.

7. Igreja Família Vitoriosa (VFC), and some other Beira churches not studied in this project, use indigenous hymnody as part of their worship experience.

locally composed. Even the majority of indigenous songs come from neighboring countries (South Africa, Tanzania, Zimbabwe, and Malawi). Some, like "Mwari Wakanaka" (God is Good), are theologically shallow due to a limited text load. Others, such as "Alvo mais que a Neve" (Whiter than Snow), clearly demonstrate a lack of critical contextualization, using poetic vocabulary and images that are nonexistent in the tropical climate of Mozambique.

PURPOSE AND GOAL

The primary purpose of this research was to explore the impact of indigenous hymnody and contextual worship arts on the development of church ministry and mission in Beira, Mozambique. The subsequent goal of this study was to discover ways to expand the songwriting workshop model for enhancing culturally appropriate worship in the local churches, thus engaging disciples and encouraging church growth.

SIGNIFICANCE

Critically contextualized worship helps the Mozambican church find the fulcrum of cultural redemption, neither falling prey to syncretism nor completely abandoning indigenous values (and uncritically embracing Western Christian culture). In addition, culturally appropriate ministry methods that foster sustainable ministries will encourage the development of a strong indigenous local church.

The globalization of missions highlights the need to reconfigure how mission is done. This study suggests new ways of doing ministry and missions by including the important components of indigenous hymnody and contextualized worship arts, as well as elevating self-theologizing while connecting to the global hermeneutical community. Within the sub-discipline of ethnomusicology in mission, refining the songwriting workshop method with the inclusion of ethnographic research and adaptive change processes helps ethnodoxologists take the next step in ministry praxis.

CENTRAL RESEARCH ISSUE

The aim of this research project was to explore the impact of indigenous hymnody and contextual worship arts on the development of church ministry and missions in selected urban church contexts in Beira, Mozambique, and to discover ways to expand the songwriting workshop model for enhancing culturally appropriate worship in the local church.

RESEARCH QUESTIONS

The following research questions guided my research:

1. What are central Mozambican cultural values of music and the arts, and how are these expressed (both historically and presently) in ministry and missions?

2. What is the present state of the local church context (on an individual and corporate level) particularly evidenced through worship praxis?

3. How can adaptive change in worship praxis be contextualized in order to reframe songwriting workshops in ways that reflect Mozambican cultural values of music and arts and emerging interests of churches, pastors, and worship leaders?

4. What kind of change in worship praxis took place as a result of this adaptive change process? How have ministry and mission been affected?

DEFINITION OF TERMS

For the purposes of this study I define the following terms:

- Church ministry: "Ministry" refers to the activities that happen at a church during Sunday services specifically focused on developing believers in the congregation, and to the discipleship that occurs through Sunday school, Bible studies, or small groups during the week.

- Contextual worship arts: Engaging the community of believers in glorifying God through the use of various cultural art forms (including but not limited to music) in critically contextualized ways. In the Mozambican context, worship arts refers primarily to music, dance, and occasionally drama (visual arts is a growing field and not commonly used within the evangelical church context in Beira, Mozambique).

- Culturally appropriate worship: Relevant worship that speaks from the heart of local believers in a local church community to the heart of God. It is what Cherry defines as convergence worship, that is, "the combining of the historical and the contemporary at every level of worship to create maximum opportunities for engaging worshippers with the presence of God."[8]

- Disciple(ship): A person who is becoming like Christ, as a student or apprentice, by following Him. Discipleship, then, is the transforming process of growth, where we meet and dwell with Jesus and his Father, empowered by the Holy Spirit, to build the Kingdom of God by participating in the *Missio Dei*.

- Indigenous hymnody: Worship songs often composed in a vernacular language with an indigenous song-form. Songs that have life and connect on a heart level with a particular people group. Tom Avery, in his article entitled "Music of the Heart" states, "The heart music of a people is usually the traditional music of that group, it is the music which they have heard and participated in as children and young people. . . . It speaks most profoundly to the emotions . . . and is usually the most expressive."[9]

- Local church: A body of believers in a given context that takes up the responsibility of congregational discipleship and continued evangelization and church planting. It may also fit Anderson and Venn's "three-self" definition of indigenous churches that describes churches that are self-propagating, self-governing, and self-supporting, though in many cases local churches are still connected to the founding mission or denomination to some degree.[10]

- Mission(s): For the purposes of this study, "mission(s)" will refer to both local and cross-cultural evangelism/church planting;[11] activities that are designed to reach nonmembers and nonbelievers and to draw them into a relationship with God and with the church.

8. Cherry, *Worship Architect*, 248.
9. Avery, "Music of the Heart," 13–14.
10. The three principles of indigenous churches, self-supporting, self-governing, and self-propagating, were first articulated by Henry Venn and Rufus Anderson, drafted formally during an 1892 conference in Shanghai.
11. I concur with Bevans and Schroeder in equating missions with evangelization. "We believe we are justified in this equation since both can have the more general meaning of the church's ministry *ad intra* (or its work of ministry to itself, so that it can be a sign and credible witness of what it stands for) and *ad extra* (or its work outside itself, persuading people to membership or promoting the values of God's reign in the world)" (*Constants in Context*, 400).

- Music-culture: In this study, I use Titon's definition of music-culture: "A group's total involvement with music: ideas, actions, institutions, material objects, everything that has to do with music."[12]
- Songwriting workshop model: A method of composing indigenous hymnody through the use of scripture, prayer, and group composition.[13]
- Worship: I agree with John Witvliet that worship is, broadly speaking, "a divine-human gift exchange" in which people dialogue with God in word and in deed.[14] However, throughout this study, I frequently use this term as a synonym for music in worship, as this is how worship is used colloquially in Beira, where the populace thinks of worship as only the music prior to the sermon.

DELIMITATIONS

My research was delimited ecclesiastically, geographically, linguistically, theologically, and artistically in the following ways:

- Ecclesiastically, I delimited the research to twelve different evangelical Protestant churches and denominations, excluding variances considered by Mozambican evangelicals to be syncretistic sects or cults (such as the Latter Day Saints or Zionists). I did not include research into the Catholic Church, Islam, or traditional religion. Though each of these spiritual streams have certainly influenced the evangelical tradition, and are therefore noted in my literature review, a complete historical study of their worship practices is beyond the scope of this study.
- Geographically, I delimited the research to the city of Beira (and outlying suburbs), in the central province of Mozambique. It is not a study of worship practices in the rural hinterlands, nor is it a countrywide study of a particular denomination and its worship praxis. This is a localized, urban, cross-case study.
- Linguistically, this study was delimited to Portuguese (the national language of Mozambique), though worship events and new songs were often in Sena or Ndau. I did not enter the debate over the value

---

12. Titon, *Worlds of Music*, 4.
13. King, *Time to Sing!*
14. Witvliet, "Preface," in Farhadian, *Christian Worship Worldwide*, xiii.

of the use of mother-tongue compared to other regional or national languages.
- Theologically, I did not enter the debate over the application of biblical content, nor doctrine. Though I encouraged the use of scriptures for composing new songs, I did not attempt to promulgate a particular church doctrine, denomination, or spiritual agenda.
- Artistically, I delimited my research to the most common worship art forms practiced in evangelical churches in Beira (music, dance, and occasionally drama). I did not explore other art forms in this study.

ASSUMPTIONS

I approached this study with the following foundational assumptions:

- I assume the use of indigenous hymnody and contextualized worship arts play a key role in church ministry and missions, particularly in the African context where "the aim is simply to express life in all of its aspects through the medium of sound."[15]
- I assume that critical contextualization and inclusion of appropriate cultural factors are vital components of a ministry's sustainability.
- I assume that the sample of twelve selected local church contexts are sufficiently reflective of the aggregate evangelical church body in Beira, Mozambique.
- I assume that the songwriting workshop model is an appropriate method for developing indigenous hymnody.
- I assume that while adaptive change in worship praxis can be difficult to measure qualitatively, it is possible to discover indicators that point towards effectiveness of worship in fostering the development of church ministry and mission.

OVERVIEW

This qualitative research is a diachronic cross-case experimental study involving twelve evangelical Protestant churches in and around the city of Beira, Mozambique. The study included fieldwork focused on discovering the present state of local church contexts and applied adaptive

15. Bebey, *African Music*, 3.

change initiating transformation through worship praxis over the course of two years, from 2012 to 2014.

This book is presented in three parts, comprised of seven chapters. I lay the foundations for the study in the introduction, providing background information, the purpose and significance of this study, and the central research problem and questions that focused my research.

Part 1 (The Landscape) situates the research in its sociohistorical context, establishing the study's contribution to the extant literature, and the rationale for the methods used. I begin with chapter 1, describing the general context in which Beira churches reside, and detail my guiding theoretical framework in chapter 2. In chapter 3, I explain the research process I used to discover the present state of local church contexts and their worship praxis.

Part 2 (The Pasture) presents the findings and data analysis that demonstrate a lack of teaching and practice of contextualized worship arts in Beira churches. In chapter 4, I describe current worship praxis in Beira, applying Titon's music-culture performance model to church services.[16] In chapter 5, I then analyze the findings presented in chapter 4, clearly showing the impact of noncontextualized worship arts in each arena of Titon's model.

Part 3 (Grazing and Growing) depicts the experimental methods I used to stimulate adaptive change in worship praxis in Beira churches, with an assessment of the results. In chapter 6, I detail how I expanded and applied the songwriting workshop model in Beira using adaptive change methods, while chapter 7 assesses the results, showing the impact of applied contextual worship arts on the development of church ministry and mission.

Finally, in the conclusion I outline the four-arena approach to ethnodoxology, recommend areas for further research, and offer some suggestions for expanding ethnodoxology praxis. I establish the necessity of contextualized worship arts as a key component of the development of the local church and its members, encouraging personal discipleship, growing ministry, and empowering for mission.

---

16. Titon, *Worlds of Music*, 16.

PART ONE

The Landscape: Exploring Mozambican Music-Culture Values

PART ONE SITUATES THE research by describing the landscape of this study, the unique features and distinctive elements that have shaped worship praxis in Mozambican evangelical churches. It begins with chapter 1, "Mozambique's Musical Context: Multicultural Migration and Missions," relating the general context in which Beira churches reside. Chapter 2, "The Literary Lay of the Land," details my guiding theoretical framework, positioning this study within the extant literature. Chapter 3, "Forming the Fence: Research Design and Method Review," describes the research process I used to discover the present state of local church contexts and their worship praxis in Beira, Mozambique.

1

Mozambique's Musical Context: Multicultural Migration and Missions

> At 9:25 a bell rings, calling the faithful to enter the church and be seated. A pastor hands me a hymnal. The youth choir begins to sing a capella, reverently filling the air with a sense of expectation. Congregants sit quietly, some with eyes closed, preparing their hearts for an encounter with God. The service leader stands and solemnly declares, "Let's pray." The doors to the church are shut as we all bow our heads for prayer.[1]

IF YOU WERE TO listen to the city of Beira, Mozambique on a Sunday morning, you would hear an assortment of sounds, beating *batuques*,[2] clapping hands, strumming guitars, dancing feet, and singing voices, all raised in resonant celebration. Music serves as a marker, an audible clue that can lead to the discovery of the complex history and dynamic religious and cultural interactions that have formed the sonic-scape of today's urban worship context in Mozambique.

---

1. Meyers, American Board (AB) site visit, field notes, 2013–14.

2. *Batuques* are traditional Mozambican membranophones (drums)—graduated cylinders of varied sizes with one head at the largest end. They can be played with hands or sticks.

Part One: The Landscape

CONTEXT

"Ungakhonda dziwa kudabuluka iwe, nkhabe dziwa kunenda iwe" (If you don't know where you come from, you won't know where you are going).[3]

Unlike some isolated cultural groups in Africa, the peoples of Mozambique have been multicultural and linked to the broader global marketplace for centuries.[4] "From Bantu-speaking farmers and fishers to Arabic traders, Goan merchants and adventuring Europeans, Mozambique has long been a crossroads of cultures."[5] This dialectic between diverse cultures (and religions), due in large part to its geographic location on the Indian Ocean, has indelibly marked the land and its people.

Not only is Mozambique defined by its coastland, but also by its rivers that trisect the country into vastly different sociopolitical and historical zones. The city of Beira, in the province of Sofala, lies at the heart of the central region, demarcated by the River Save in the south, and the River Zambezi to the north. As Mozambique's third largest city (boasting a population of 546,000 according to the 2007 census),[6] Beira has historic significance as a land bridge connecting the African interior to the global marketplace. As it is the port city for the major sources of economic wealth in Mozambique as well as for neighboring land-locked countries, Beira remains a pivotal nexus for the nation.

---

3. Common Sena proverb. The Sena people are a major sociolinguistic group located within central Mozambique.

4. For a lengthy but fascinating historical overview of Mozambique, I highly recommend Malyn Newitt's seminal work, *History of Mozambique*.

5. Fitzpatrick, *Mozambique*, 22.

6. "List of Cities in Mozambique by Population," Wikipedia, https://en.wikipedia.org/wiki/list_of_cities_in_mozambique_by_population.

Mozambique's Musical Context: Multicultural Migration and Missions 13

Figure 1: Aerial View of Beira (Wikimedia Commons)

Contested Cultural Claims to the City

"They don't like us because they say we aren't from here ... but neither are they!"[7]

The modern city of Beira was founded in 1884 near the mouth of the Pungue River as a base of operations for Joaquim Carlos Paiva de Andrade, a wealthy *prazero* (plantation owner). The city's location in a no-man's land of alluvial swampland forced Beira's founders to employ workers from the surrounding hinterlands for house construction and domestic work. These employees were drawn primarily from two language groups, Sena and Ndau (see figures 2a and 2b below),[8] continuing to live in linguistically divided *bairros* (neighborhoods) on the town's outskirts.

---

7. Meyers, José, Sena gardner, field notes, 2012–13.

8. Other language groups found in Beira include Lomwe (Zambezi), Cistwa (Inhambane), and Shona (Zimbabwe) along with scores of others who have moved to the city for political or economic reasons.

14 Part One: The Landscape

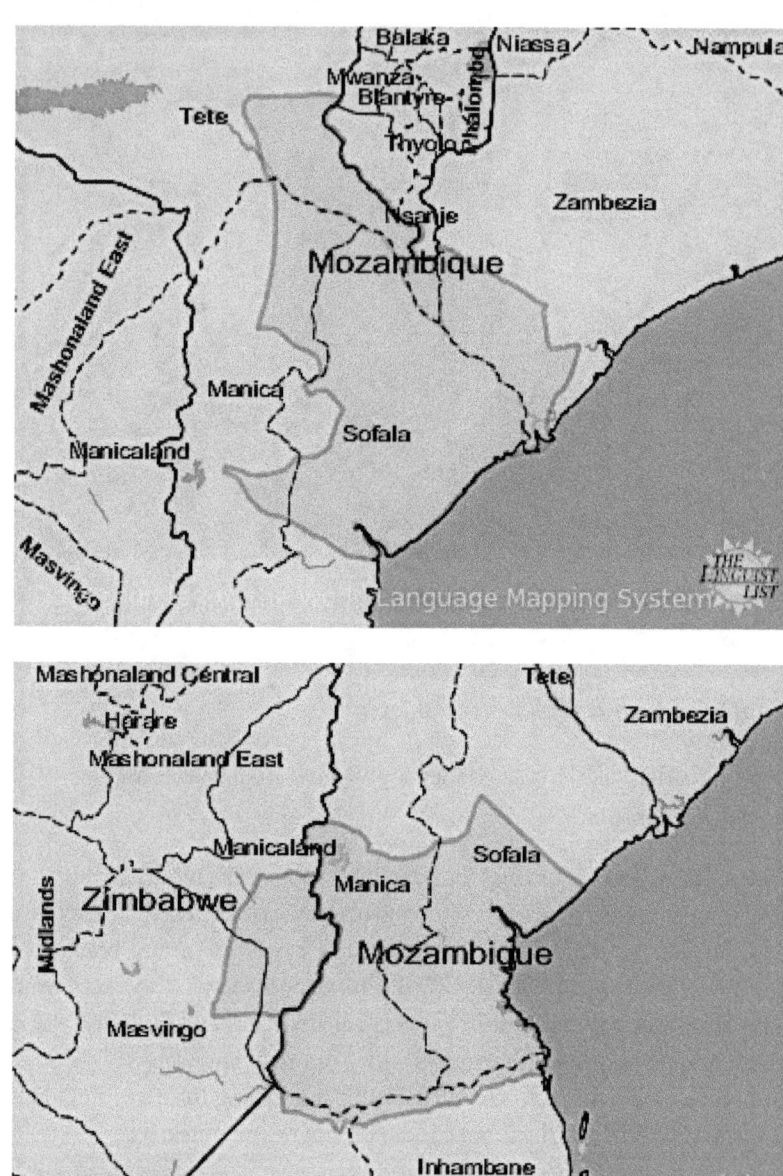

Figures 2a and 2b: Sena and Ndau Language Maps (multitree.org)

Sena and Ndau share many traditional cultural traits, but urban migration in the late 1800s and resultant linguistic interaction between these language groups formed unique cultural characteristics.[9] Unlike other Mozambican cities, Beira does not have a distinctive mono-linguistic cultural identity, and people are usually reticent to greet a stranger in dialect,[10] as one never knows who is Sena or Ndau. This hesitancy is so pronounced, it has been said that the mother tongue of *Beirenses* (habitants of Beira) is Portuguese. Though this view is not entirely correct, there are many inhabitants for whom this is true, and indicative of a cultural identity widely influenced by the surrounding global reality.

An example of this hybrid uniqueness is an emerging language, jokingly called "Mabangue," by youth, a type of pidgin that is spoken in Beira. It is an amalgamation of Portuguese, English, Sena, and Ndau with expressions such as "*vamos jobar*" (let's go to work; Portuguese "let's go," English "job" with a Portuguese "ar" verb ending).[11] Creative solutions for communication and survival, illustrated primarily through the art forms of music and dance are just some of the elusive distinctives of Beira's complex cultural characteristics.

Influence of Foreign Missions on Local Worship Praxis

"The missionaries said our music called the devil!"[12]

Beirenses encounter not only a multiplicity of languages, but also a plurality of religious traditions. Mozambican authorities estimate that there are currently more than thee hundred registered Christian denominations operating throughout the country today, including the Roman Catholic church, mainline Protestant churches, Evangelical churches, African-initiated churches (AICs), and Pentecostals.[13] When one considers the adherents to all the religions (including African traditional religions,

---

9. Both culture groups are organized in groups of families or kin, with a power structure loosely guided by traditional chiefs. Their primary economic activity is subsistence agriculture, complimented by fishing or hunting (Nhancalize, *Canção*, 17–18).

10. In Mozambique, some people refer to the indigenous languages as dialects or mother tongue, though they are not technically dialects, but languages in their own right.

11. Curiously, the Bangue people (who spoke a dialect of Ndau) were the original inhabitants of the land surrounding Beira, though their language and culture have long been overwhelmed by the urban migration described above.

12. Meyers, field notes, 2013–14.

13. Massicame, "Ecumenism in Mozambique," 410.

ATRs), one could say that to be Mozambican is to be religious; and to be religious is to worship.

In Table 1, I show the percentages of adherents to the major religions present in Mozambique according to the 2007 census. I used Bevans and Schroeder's three-type theology as a reference for Table 1, although their brief sketch of AICs and Pentecostalism could do with a more comprehensive treatment, especially when considering the phenomenal growth of "indigenous Christianity," which (while rooted in Type A) evades the neat "pigeon-holing" of early missions movements.[14] They understandably, but unfortunately, do not cover Islam.

I also use James Krabill's stages of musical development—importation, adaptation, alteration, imitation, indigenization, and internationalization—to describe the worship styles of the various religions in Mozambique.[15] In the importation stage, hymn tunes, texts, and rhythms all originate with the Western missionary. Imported hymn tunes or texts are, in some way, "Africanized" in the adaptation stage, therefore rendering them more suitable and intelligible to worshippers in a given setting.

The alteration stage takes it a step further and some part of the missionary's hymn (tune, text, or rhythm) is replaced or significantly modified by an indigenous form. Tunes, texts, and rhythms are locally composed but in a style that replicates a Western musical genre in the imitation stage. In the indigenization stage, tunes, texts, and rhythms are locally produced in indigenous musical forms and styles. Finally, in the internationalization stage, tunes, texts, and rhythms from the global faith family beyond the west and one's own local context become incorporated into the life and worship of the church.

---

14. Bevans and Schroeder, *Constants in Context*, 265–56, 272–75.

15 Krabill, as cited in King, *Music in the Life*, 57–80.

Table 1: Comparison of Religions in Mozambique

Religion	Arrival in Moz.	Geographic Location	Adherents[16]	Theology Type	Worship Style
Traditional		Throughout	18.7%		Indigenization
Islam	12th c.	North	17.9%		Importation Adaptation
Catholic	1498	Central	28.4%	A/C	Importation Adaptation Indigenization
Protestant	Late 1800s	South	12.2%	A/C	Importation Adaptation Alteration
Zionist	Early 1900s	Throughout	15.5%	A	Indigenization

Key: A: Mission as saving souls and extending the church; C: Mission as commitment to liberation and transformation; A/C: Both theologies, Worship Style: Krabill's stages of musical development

Though over half of Mozambicans are Christian as a result of decades of mission efforts, a mission history of a largely noncontextualized gospel is blatantly obvious in current worship praxis. Notable exceptions include the White Fathers,[17] who practiced a theology of adaptation (now known as contextualization), and the Mozambican Catholic church since independence that incorporates contextual worship arts into the liturgy. Though some types of AICs (like Zionists) are criticized as being syncretistic, their explosive growth over the last few decades, with their distinctly African charismatic expressions, testifies to the power of contextualized worship. However, the majority of mainline Protestant churches and many evangelical Pentecostals today still struggle with the burden of an imported worship style.

---

16. The percentage of Protestant adherents, according to the CIA World Fact Book, based on the 2007 census, include Anglicans (1.3 percent) and Evangelicals/Pentecostals (10.9 percent). In the 2007 census, the option "none" had animistic as a descriptor. Therefore, I have designated the CIA's "none" category as traditional adherents above.

17. The "White Fathers" (so named because their habit resembles the robes of Algerian Arabs) are a Roman Catholic missionary society, also known as the Society of Missionaries of Africa.

SUMMARY

Regardless of religion and mission history, we sing our faith, and it is out of this axiom that my research emerged. I wanted to discover how contextually appropriate worship affected discipleship within and beyond the local church, how Mozambicans "grazed and grew" through music. With the diverse linguistic and religious context within which the Mozambican urban church resides in mind, I now turn to the missiological and theoretical framework that directed my research.

2

The Literary Lay of the Land

As the leader calls out the name of a parish group, they start to sing as they rhythmically process down the center aisle to give their monthly offering. Others in the youth choir and audience join in the song.

When the group reaches the offering basket set on a table at the front of the sanctuary, the lead dancer puts the parish offering envelope with the collected total in the basket. The group continues to sing and begins dancing around the table.

Some break out into a special jumping dance, joyfully celebrating the blessing of giving. Clapping, ululation, and shouts encourage the dancers, while others, spurred on by the enthusiasm, throw coins into the milieu.[1]

MUSIC EVENTS ARE COMPLICATED ethnographic phenomena that defy quick and easy descriptions. Thorough understanding requires a multidisciplinary approach, carefully analyzing the manifold elements that comprise the whole performance. In this chapter I review the missiological and theoretical foci that furthered this research and facilitated comprehension.

---

1. Meyers, Evangelho Completo de Deus (ECD) site visit, field notes, 2013–14.

MISSIOLOGY

> Culture is the workplace of Christian theology.[2]

While up until the latter quarter of the last century anthropology was not considered necessary for missionary training, today one would be hard-pressed to find a missions agency that does not include some component of cultural training. In fact, one could argue that "no one would be considered adequately trained for cross-cultural missions now without some understanding of cultural anthropology."[3]

This shift is a welcome change to how missions had been done, and a much needed corrective that addresses the growing issue of "split-level" Christianity, a term first coined by Father Jaime Bulatao ("Split-Level Christianity"), and further developed by Paul Hiebert in his writings on critical contextualization in *Understanding Folk Religion*. Rather than simply deny or condemn the existence of folk religious beliefs and practices, missionaries with anthropological training can consciously apply the process of critical contextualization within their missional setting.

Critical Contextualization

> Without contextualization, people will not connect to Christ in a way that moves their hearts. Faith will feel foreign.[4]

What exactly is critical contextualization? Kraft states that contextualization is simply "the process of learning to express genuine Christianity in socioculturally appropriate ways."[5] Flemming concurs, affirming that it is "how the gospel revealed in Scripture authentically comes to life in each new culture."[6] It is not simply indigenization; rather, it "suggests a far more comprehensive and profound process of accommodating the gospel to the total life of a people."[7] Haleblian broadens the scope, describing contextualization as "that discipline which deals with the essential nature

---

2. Walls, *Missionary Movement*, 3.
3. Hiebert, *Anthropological Reflections*, 9.
4. Moreau, *Contextualization in World Missions*, 18–19.
5. Kraft, *Anthropology for Christian Witness*, 376.
6. Flemming, *Contextualization in New Testament*, 13–14.
7. Bosch, "Split-Level Christianity," 495.

of the gospel, its cross-cultural communication and the development and fostering of local theologies and indigenous church forms."[8]

While definitions of contextualization abound, the essential goal remains "to frame the gospel message in language and communication forms appropriate and meaningful to the local culture and to focus the message upon crucial issues in the lives of people."[9] This is a narrow road, a path that lies between syncretism and an uncritical embrace of Western Christian culture, a road that leads beyond contextualization to a more global "metatheology." Hiebert postulates, "Ironically, this metatheological process, carried out on the international level, may lead us to what Western theologians have long sought, a growing consensus on theological absolutes. It may bring us closer to the formulation of a truly supracultural theology."[10]

There are, perhaps, as many approaches to contextualization as there are definitions. These methods vary, in part, due to their view of the roles of biblical text and context. Moreau divides these positions into two camps. He titles the first "translation," that is, the idea that Scripture is the message, and that missionaries must find the cultural bridge to communicate. The second he calls "existential," that missionaries should discover and come alongside what God is already doing in culture.[11]

I would argue, along with Moreau, that both text and context are critical and that effective contextualization must address the following seven dimensions: doctrinal/philosophical, ethical/legal, mythic/narrative, social/organizational, ritual, experiential/supernatural, and material/artistic.[12] In other words, the point of contextualization is a complete transformation of the individual and their context. "Scripture should penetrate every aspect of society and transform every part of culture. All church life and Christian living should reflect scriptural truth in clear and compelling ways. Contextualization must be comprehensive."[13]

While contextualization in theory is appealing, it can also run amok, particularly by the third and fourth generation of believers, becoming an inert holy huddle. Indigenization, if left unchecked, can lead

---

8. Haleblian, "Problem of Contextualization," 97.
9. Lingenfelter, *Transforming Culture*, 12.
10. Hiebert, *Anthropological Reflections*, 103.
11. Moreau, "Contextualization," 321–48.
12. Moreau, "Contextualization that is Comprehensive," 324–35.
13. Ibid., 284–85.

to syncretistic stagnation and even church death. In contrast, a church focused on other-worldliness, looking to the universal principles of the faith and seeking obedience to Christ and the Scriptures can miss connecting to local realities. The balance lies in the tension between what Andrew Walls describes as the "indigenizing principle" and the "pilgrim principle."[14] Sherwood Lingenfelter goes so far as to state boldly:

> The contradiction between the pilgrim principle . . . and the indigenous principle . . . is implicit in all church ministries. Indigenous churches . . . result from effective contextualization. While in their formation they serve as a powerful force for spreading the gospel, they may become a vehicle of compromise and death. The pilgrim principle, connecting local believers to the universal church with a vision for outreach to the world, provides a necessary counterbalance.[15]

This low view of culture differs from earlier anthropological missiologists. Culture is not merely neutral, but actively working to "squeeze people into its mold."[16] I concur with Lingenfelter in advocating not just a transference but a transformation of culture by first recognizing our own cultural prison and the cultural prisons of others, and by then leading a pilgrim life of submission to one another in Christ.[17]

The advantage of exploring contextual worship arts is that it, by nature, encompasses all seven of Moreau's dimensions. When people worship, they sing their doctrine, they reflect how they think about the world and how they should live. Singing collectively, they show their sense of togetherness in repeated symbolic actions of their faith, and they sense the presence of God. Worship, finally, is expressed in artistic form. It is, as Roberta King argues, our "sung theology."[18]

Songwriting workshops use Scripture as the inspiration for lyrics, but also reflect on the contextual reality, looking past the text and into the culture. The context raises questions and issues that need biblical answers in song, the context helps us communicate in ways beyond words, the context even reveals "redemptive analogies" as well as cultural blind

---

14. Walls, "Gospel As the Prisoner," 97–99.
15. Lingenfelter, *Transforming Culture*, 15.
16. Ibid.
17. Ibid., 176.
18. King, *Time to Sing!*, 117–18.

spots.[19] While this method yields results, the challenge is always to avoid stagnation, to find the balance between indigenization and pilgrimage. This research, then, takes a critical view of culture, seeking to comprehensively contextualize worship arts in a way that will affect life-long transformation in Mozambican pilgrims.

Worship

> In liturgy (worship), God acts to empower the church for mission.[20]

An important yet often neglected area of missiology is the significance of worship. John Piper in his book *Let the Nations be Glad!* argues that worship is, in fact, "the ultimate goal of the church (not missions)."[21] Bevans and Schroeder further develop Piper's contention by stating:

> The church is most the church when it is assembled for worship; the Christian is most a Christian when he or she is in attentive dialogue with God; prayer and liturgy are the *center* of Christian life, and yet that center will only hold if Christian eyes are not on the center but on its periphery . . . to encounter God at the center is to participate in God's life at the boundaries; to participate in God's boundary-crossing mission is to be drawn always to the center.[22]

One cannot be missional without being in communion with God through worship, and one cannot worship without also being drawn into the rhythm of God's missional heartbeat.

These authors make a compelling case for the interlocking dependence of worship on mission, and mission on worship. In fact, Simon Chan contends that "Eucharistic worship does not end in cozy fellowship, but in costly mission to the world."[23] Indeed it does. Yet many churches and mission agencies still divorce one from the other, impoverishing both their missional impulse and their worship.

Considering the essential nature of worship in missions, it is distressing that worship is not assigned a more central position in

---

19. This concept comes from Don Richardson's books *Peace Child* and *Eternity in Their Hearts*.
20. Bevans and Schroeder, *Constants in Context*, 362.
21. Piper, *Let the Nations be Glad!*, 11.
22. Bevans and Schroeder, *Constants in Context*, 362.
23. Chan, "Mother Church," 189.

theological training and missional work. Robert Webber criticizes our lack of training:

> Seminary education does not equip a pastor for leading worship. Many seminaries do not even require worship courses or training. The training that pastors do get is in the art of preaching.... Unfortunately, because of this training and perhaps even because of their gifts, most pastors feel that preaching is the essence of worship. A few outstanding and gifted preachers build the church around their preaching and feel they are quite successful at it, but this is neither biblical nor is it, in the end, a means to good worship.[24]

Evangelical Christians suffer from what Sally Morgenthaler calls a "sermon fixation."[25] Her work, *Worship Evangelism*, offers a similar critique to Piper's, commenting:

> We must come to terms with this truth: Although evangelism is one of the central tasks of the church, it is worship that "drives" evangelism, not vice-versa.... The true goal of evangelism is to produce more and better worshippers.... Worship... is the ultimate purpose of the church and has been since its beginning.[26]

J. Nathan Corbitt broadens the scope, arguing that kingdom music can play not just the role of the evangelist, but also the roles of priest, prophet, proclaimer, healer, preacher, and teacher. While he speaks specifically about music, one can infer a larger sense of the word, alluding to worship. He states:

> Music is essential in the total life of Christians and Christian communities around the world. Christianity is a singing and musical faith. From the remotest village common to the center urban stage, Christian musicians seek to share their song and to learn from those in other parts of the kingdom. Music is a servant of the church and a tool for its servants.[27]

Why have Christians neglected such a powerful tool? Is it so ubiquitous that we don't even recognize its presence and its power to transform lives? In the African context, where "music is life," it is a tool for transformation that the church cannot afford to neglect. Worship must resume

---

24. Webber, *Signs of Wonder*, 25.
25. Morgenthaler, *Worship Evangelism*, 43.
26. Ibid., 38, 39, 43.
27. Corbitt, *Sound of the Harvest*, 18.

its rightful place on center stage, and once again become the main focus in churches, in seminaries, and in the lives of believers.

The question remains, what type of worship is needed? Is it simply enough to proclaim Scriptures and sing the songs we've always sung, to continue to repeat the hymns missionaries brought along with the gospel? I contend that it is not. Becoming a Christian is not equivalent to cultural genocide vis-à-vis musical forms.[28] That is hardly good news to new converts. Rather, the gospel reaches into new contexts, transforming people and cultures, inspiring new songs that, in turn, evangelize others.[29]

If worship is, in essence, a "divine-human gift exchange"[30] in which we experience the gospel of the incarnate Christ, then it must be contextualized. One cannot freely encounter God, nor unreservedly convey one's newfound faith through foreign worship expressions. True worship speaks from our hearts to the heart of God; it is a dialogue, God revealing, and humans responding in word and in deed. Engendering true worship through contextualization is the goal of ethnodoxology.

Ethnodoxology

Ethnodoxology = Peoples + Praise[31]

Having briefly explored the importance of both comprehensive contextualization and worship in missiology, I now turn to the discipline of ethnodoxology, that is, the *trialogue*[32] of anthropology, musicology, and missiology. Music and arts in mission did not really enter the Western evangelical world until the 1960s when Vida Chenowith began working on concepts for missionary musicians through her work in Papua New Guinea. Shortly thereafter, Roberta King and Joyce Scott started making analogous ministry efforts on the continent of Africa.

Their influence quickly spread, and by the 1980s many international missions agencies began advancing the call for worship and arts in mission. David Hall first coined the term "ethnodoxology" in a series

---

28. Masa, "Future of African Music," 157.
29. King, *Time to Sing!*, 2–3.
30. Witvliet, *Christian Worship Worldwide*, xiii.
31. As defined on the International Council of Ethnodoxologists home page, www.worldofworship.org.
32. This term is used by Harvie Conn in his book, *Eternal Word and Changing Worlds*.

of theological articles written in the mid 1990s, and in 1996, the *Mission Frontiers* landmark issue featuring ethnodoxology prompted the formation of several new arts ministries. This late-bloomer focus of music and the arts in mission has continued to crescendo.[33]

King's four-fold matrix for studies in ethnomusicology and the Christian faith calls for an integration of the discipline of ethnomusicology within missiology. This model advocates comprehensive contextualization through worship.[34] "Music-in-Culture and the Missional Context," the first domain of study, reminds us that music cultures are organized differently; they are dynamic and always changing. One's own musical ethnocentrism should never impede effective communication of the gospel through music. The second domain, "Music-in-Culture and the Biblical Text," communicates the gospel message with music that is understood by people within their local setting. Theological reflection through song promotes knowing God in context. One must ask the question, "What does the music mean to the receptor?"

"Music Makers and Personal Pilgrimage," the third domain, calls for Christian musicians to be grounded in biblical knowledge, spiritual formation, spiritual disciplines, and theological reflection. Musicians must be provided the space and opportunity to develop musical skills and practice composing songs for the church. Church leadership must encourage a theology and philosophy of music that fosters good decision-making and leadership related to Christian music in the church.

The final domain, "Music-in-Culture and the Faith Community," respects each group of people within the church and their musical languages and traditions. As a local body of believers pursues developing and employing music that builds the faith of Christian believers, Christian community is formed through hermeneutical new song fellowships or composer's clubs.

As comprehensive contextualization is critical to successful transformation and discipleship of believers, I intentionally used King's four-fold matrix as a guiding framework that shaped both my methodology and data analysis of local church ministries and missions in the context of Beira, Mozambique. I explored the surrounding cultural context, used Scriptures as inspirations for song texts, built relationships with worship leaders and pastors, and worked within local churches to encourage the

---

33. Fortunato and Harris, "Crescendo of Local Arts," 113–18.
34. King, *Music in the Life*, 293–301.

development of contextual worship arts for discipleship. This multi-pronged approach to applied ethnodoxology proved to be an effective means of initiating adaptive change in worship praxis. I return to a discussion of King's matrix in the conclusion of this study.

As stated previously, due to the pulpit fixation that plagues most theological training, African ethnodoxology literature is extremely limited. Hence, I must turn to the academic work conducted primarily outside of the disciplines of theology and worship, that of ethnomusicology.

THEORETICAL FRAMES FROM ETHNOMUSICOLOGY

> Oluadah Equiano, a former slave wrote: "We are almost without a doubt, a nation of dancers, musicians and poets. Thus every great event is celebrated with public dances, which are accompanied with songs and dances suited to the occasion."[35]

I begin this section by briefly exploring music's role in African culture as viewed through the lens of Africanist Ethnomusicology over the course of the last century. I then discuss pop music, postmodernity, and power, nascent issues endemic in an urban environment. Finally, I turn to the disciplines of communication and ritual performance that aided me in the analysis of church music events.

Africanist Ethnomusicology

> "Music is life!" (Pastor João)[36]

One can argue that Africanist ethnomusicology began eighteen years after the Berlin Conference dividing Africa among the European powers (1884–85), with the collaborative work of Hornbostel, Abraham, and linguists in analyzing the relationship of speech tone and melody in Ewe songs from Togo. "However, the field and its core concerns were not systematically defined until a quarter of a century later in Hornbostel's 1928 article, "African Negro Music," published in the first issue of the ethnological journal *Africa*."[37]

---

35. Southern, *Music of Black Africans*, 6–7.
36. Meyers, field notes, 2012–13.
37. Waterman, "Uneven Development," 169.

Much has changed in the following eight decades from the initial historical, areal, and diffusionist approaches,[38] now largely viewed as problematic, and early rhythmic studies.[39] There has been a rise in the number of African scholars and specialists in African music,[40] and the emergence of other schools of theory and method including the study of popular music, applied ethnomusicology, and researcher reflexivity.[41]

Considering that sub-Saharan Africa is an enormous, diverse land mass inhabited by more than 500 million people speaking over eight hundred languages, the current resistance to ethnographic generalization is appropriate. "Kwabena Nketia's cautious characterization of African music as 'a network of distinct yet related traditions which overlap in certain aspects of style, practice or usage' probably indicates the current limits of reasonable generalization."[42]

While much ethnographic research includes analysis of aspects of traditional religions, as most African music and arts play a spiritual role, ethnomusicologists have shied away from exploring church or worship music.[43] In fact, Michelle Kisliuk's fieldwork experience among the BaAka of the effects of missionizing efforts, particularly in relation to worship praxis, were quite negative. She recounts:

> In 1989 ... I encountered the effects of recent missionizing efforts by evangelists from the Grace Brethren Church. An American woman, named Barbara ... focused her "church-planting" work on a permanent BaAka settlement, called Dzanga.... I tried to keep an open mind, but when I got to Dzanga I could not help but be shocked and saddened by what I saw. The BaAka there had completely stopped performing the current repertoire

---

38. Jones, *Studies in African Music*; Merriam, "African Music"; Wachsmann, "Human Migration"; Lomax, "Homogeneity of African–Afro-American Musical Style."

39. Tracey, *Chopi Musicians*; Blacking, "Eight Flute Tunes"; Chernoff, *African Rhythm*.

40. Nketia, *Music of Africa*; Bebey, *African Music*; Chitando, *Singing Culture*; Agawu, *Representing African Music*; Kidula, *Music in Kenyan Christianity*.

41. Berliner, *Soul of Mbira*; Stone, *Let the Inside Be Sweet*; Waterman, *Juju*; King, *Time to Sing*; Scott, *Tuning In*; Meintjes, *Sound of Africa*; Barz, *Singing for Life*; Titon, *Worlds of Music*.

42. Waterman, "Africa," 240. As space does not permit me to elucidate, I refer the reader to the excellent review of African ethnomusicological literature by Waterman in chapter 7 of the 1993 Norton/Grove Handbooks in Music, *Ethnomusicology: Historical and Regional Studies*.

43. A notable exception to this is Shelemay's work on Orthodox Christian music in Ethiopia (Shelemay, "Zema").

> of music and dance forms. . . . (They) had been convinced by (the missionary) that their own music, dance, and traditional medicine were "satanic." The BaAka told me proudly, assuming that I would approve since I am white . . . that they now only sing hymns to the Christian god in "church." These hymns were not in their own language. . . . What I saw and heard then looked to me like a slavish imitation of the missionaries, like a kind of cultural genocide.[44]

This account is a painful reminder of the regrettable effects of noncontextualized mission efforts, and a resounding affirmation of the necessity of including sound ethnographic research in conjunction with ministry endeavors in African churches today.

Thus, this contextually applied research sits at the intersection of the work of secular ethnomusicologists and the ministry of music missionaries; conducting an ethnographic analysis of local Mozambican churches and their worship praxis, then collaborating with pastors and worship leaders to develop contextualized worship arts that result in positive, authentic transformation on an individual and collective basis. There is, however, another layer of complexity that must be considered when exploring churches in the urban context, that is, the interplay of pop music, postmodernity, and power.

Pop Music, Postmodernity, and Power

> Musical appropriation sings a double line with one voice (one line is admiration the other is appropriation).[45]

Urban dwellers are faced with a befuddling complexity of competing ideas and identities, epitomized by the dizzying array and proliferation of musical options. Timothy Taylor, in his seminal work *Global Pop: World Music, World Markets*, argues that "nothing better exemplifies this new world . . . and the changes in it than music, for the very malleability of music makes possible local appropriations and alterations . . . resulting in all kinds of syncretisms and hybridities."[46] In fact, pop music is so globally ubiquitous, it has resulted in what Simon Frith calls a "universal pop

---

44. Kisliuk, "(Un)Doing Fieldwork," 189–90.
45. Feld, "Notes on World Beat," 238.
46. Taylor, *Global Pop*, xv.

aesthetic."[47] The pervasiveness of pop music elevates current musical and theoretical issues more than perhaps any other cultural form, and must not be neglected by African music academics.[48]

It almost goes without saying that worship music in a city church is most often a type of pop music phenomena, and a product of its urban environment. Music sung in churches is meant to appeal to the entire congregation; specifically performed to elicit audience participation by affirming one's faith through song. Resources and technology available in the urban context, such as electricity, Western instruments, and internet access, impact what songs are sung and how they are performed. Therefore, attention must be given to the nascent context of this music-culture, the city, and how the effects of globalization influence the creation and proliferation of pop worship music; how identity and community are shaped through song.

While Copelan's work on urban music began the discussion of musicians as culture brokers, "the study of music-makers as social actors remains an underdeveloped branch of Africanist ethnomusicology."[49] In fact, ethnomusicology as a whole at that time had spent little time addressing urban music cultures, concentrating instead on rural environments. Yet, following anthropology's lead in the 1960s, ethnomusicologists have increasingly moved their research to the cities.[50]

Previous fieldwork often provided a sampling of the entire repertory of the music of a given culture, seeing it in its entirety as a system. "This same approach was not, however, followed in studying the music of the cities. The reason is, no doubt, that the musical "system" of a city is far more complex, defying quick comprehension."[51] Nettl suggests instead that urban ethnomusicologists should focus on analyzing the interaction and cross-pollination of a multitude of music genres/styles, a unique characteristic of urban music, specifically popular music. "In the cities of the developing and recently developed world, popular music has become

---

47. Frith, "Introduction, World Music," 2.

48. Notable exceptions being Christopher Waterman's work on juju music (*Juju: A Social History and Ethnography of an African Popular Music*), Stapleton and May's *African Rock*, and Phillip Bohlman's comprehensive, *World Music: A Very Short Introduction*.

49. Waterman, "Africa," 252.

50. See Turino's excellent work on Thomas Mapfumo's pop music of the 1980s in urban Zimbabwe (2000).

51. Nettl, *Eight Urban Music Cultures*, 8.

one of the main sources of both musical change and the combining of musical styles" and has, therefore, special importance as a sociocultural phenomenon.[52] This is particularly true in Beira, where *nossa música* (our music), itself a hybridity, is the most popular genre of church music in the churches studied.[53]

Postmodernity and increasing urbanization have wrought significant social changes. Manuel states:

> For many, the changes ... are accompanied by considerable alienation, exploitation, and impoverishment. As such, the creation of a new social identity assumes a crucial rather than incidental role in survival and adaptation to the new environment. To those immersed in the struggle, popular music may serve as a powerful and meaningful symbol of identity, functioning as an avenue of expression and mediation of conflict. Popular music, however much it may sound to the naïve ear as a crude imitation of other forms, may serve as a metaphor for the creation of a distinctive world of common meanings and shared cultural ideologies on the part of the new urban classes.[54]

The rapid growth in cities often brings together members of distinct ethnic and linguistic origins. Thus, as Manuel has noted, we can observe that where peoples interact with each other, popular music plays a mediating role, forming and expressing the reorientation of social identity that inevitably occurs in the urban environment.

Victor Turner argues that these liminal or transitional groups have a strong sense of social identity. "Usually they are highly conscious and self-conscious people and may produce from their ranks a disproportionately high number of writers, artists, and philosophers."[55] In the church setting, music not only mediates between people, but also between the congregation and God; it is a liminal bridge between humans and the Divine. This research explores church music associated with particular social groupings; in this instance, comparing and contrasting twelve cases to better understand the reality of worship praxis in urban context of Beira, Mozambique.

---

52. Ibid., 12.

53. Out of the 154 songs analyzed from nine different churches, 103 songs were *nossa música* style, roughly two-thirds of the music studied.

54. Manuel, *Popular Music*, 16–17.

55. Turner, *Dramas, Fields and Metaphors*, 233.

Popular music is always a music form in flux, caught between many worlds. John Roberts contends:

> In reality the issue of "authenticity" is largely irrelevant in popular music.... Some of their most "typical" styles are the result of cross-fertilization from overseas.... Long-term examination of any area's music suggests an ebb and flow between indigenous and foreign influences.[56]

This is certainly true in the context of Beira. I quickly realized that, while admirable, a rigid attempt to create authentic indigenous hymnody may well be unappreciated by those I was trying to serve, and could well be yet another form of foreign worship oppression.

I had to critically reflect on how my presence and position influenced my relationships with others. While Hiebert briefly outlines as one of the stress points the nature of the shape of the relationship between missionaries and nationals, he omits the underlying issue of power and positionality.[57] Ministry is rarely a level playing field, and the bicultural bridge upon which interpersonal cross-cultural relationships are formed is often slanted in favor of the missionaries.[58]

The challenge for this research was not only to apply comprehensive contextualization to theology, missiology, and ecclesiology but also to critically reflect on the wider urban culture itself. I asked the questions: What does it mean to be a Christian in Beira? How does a *Beirense* (someone from the city of Beira) uniquely worship God? Defining a music-culture identity became an important part of composing contextual worship music in the city of Beira, Mozambique.

In today's reality, "everyone is a scatterling, everyone is displaced ... left without a stable home or identity."[59] This global displacement puts all of us "on the road" and in contact with each other in new ways. We are all pilgrims and cocreators. These interactions give us an opportunity for creative collaboration. It is as we walk, worshipping together, as "companions of the road"[60] in search of shalom, that we begin to see true transformation occur.

---

56. Roberts, *Latin Tinge*, 23.
57. Hiebert, *Anthropological Reflections*, 147.
58. See Hiebert, "The Bicultural Bridge" in *Anthropological Reflections*, 147–58, for further details.
59. Taylor, *Global Pop*, 181.
60. Linnea Boese, a dear friend, mentor, and missionary in Ivory Coast, uses this

Communication through Ritual Performance

> The practice of local assemblies is thus a primary referent ... of the church's understanding of its ritual life. Within each local setting, faith and culture are inseparable.[61]

Church services, using multiple forms of human expression, are complex music events to study. Mary McGann affirms:

> In worship a community uses various modes of communication and interaction to enact the ritual, movements, sound, gestures, speech, musical idioms, objects, dress, time, space, light and color. These complex forms of communication, sometimes referred to as the "languages" of ritual action, coalesce in a total expressive system. . . . Therefore, these various modes of communication require careful attention, since they act simultaneously and forcefully in how a community makes meaning.[62]

Each language of ritual action then, must be understood not only on its own terms as a medium of cultural meaning, but also in how it relates to and gives meaning to the ritual in its entirety. Does it complement or compete with other "languages" used in the liturgical event?

The field of communication theory is helpful when analyzing a music event, as music is a means of communicating individual and social identity. Thomas Turino states, "The crucial link between identity formation and arts like music lies in the specific semiotic character of these activities which make them particularly affective and direct ways of knowing."[63]

This field, known as musical semiotics, or the "study of music as a sign and as communication,"[64] is an entire sub-field of ethnomusicology that has gained momentum in the last few decades, with the works of Earo Tarasti and Turino. While semiotics is indeed fascinating, the

---

phrase when addressing partners in ministry. It is a direct translation of a Nyarafolo expression, *kodan?any&ni.* (road-walking-mate). I appreciate the sentiment that we are a traveling hermeneutical community—the universal church journeying toward shalom.

61. McGann, *Exploring Music*, 16.
62. Ibid., 20.
63. Turino, "Signs of Imagination," 221.
64. Tarasti, *Signs of Music*, v.

field is far too esoteric for the purposes of this research of applied ethnodoxology.

The more "user-friendly" transactional model of communication, first put forth by D. C. Barnlund in 1970,[65] enables an analysis of the relationship between the source, message, and receptor, and process of "meaning bargaining" that occurs during a performance.[66] It implies an ongoing transaction between the source and receptor, that the message is fluid and permeable, malleable by both the source and receptor.

King effectively used the transactional model of communication in her research, relating it to music events of the Senufo of Côte d'Ivoire. According to King, everyone who is involved in the music-making event is a participant. There are designated initiator and interactant participants, but all respond and create meaning together. Four communication channels are present—music sound, song texts, dance movements, and kinesic symbolism—and the performers that facilitate the event. Communication transactions occur through these four channels. "Thus it is that meaning is something that is assigned or given to a communication event rather than something merely sent and received."[67]

These communication channels are also present in the Beira church context, and participation by all present is expected. "Bargaining for meaning" occurs across each of these channels. Communication is fluid and flexible. The transactional model of communication concept, therefore, was an implicit undergirding paradigm that supported my research throughout.

Performance ethnography, or performative anthropology, pioneered by Victor Turner and Richard Schechner in the 1970s, proved to be an effective method conducive to gaining understanding about the interactive complexity of ritual languages and communication channels in the music event of church services.

Kisliuk affirms this approach, arguing that a focus on the "ethnography of performance" through participation is critical.[68] "Because of our participation in performance, ethnomusicologists are especially aware that there is much one can only know by doing."[69] By becoming

65. Barnlund, "Transactional Model," 42–57.
66. King, *Pathways in Christian Music*, 58.
67. Ibid.
68. Kisliuk, "(Un)Doing Fieldwork," 183.
69. Ibid., 33. Space and time do not permit me to elucidate further into this rather recent and exciting development in anthropology. For more

part of the ritual performance, I gained insider information about the relationship between the source, the message, and the receptors through reflexive processing, and bargaining for meaning with the other performers and the audience.

SUMMARY

In this chapter I explored the missiological and theoretical frameworks that directed my research, demonstrating that neither missiology nor ethnomusicology have adequately addressed Christian urban worship praxis. This study, then, sits at the crossroads between the work of secular ethnomusicologists and the ministry of music missionaries. I now move to describe the research process, explaining the research design and methods used throughout this study.

---

information, I refer the reader to an excellent overview, "On the Road to a New Ethnography: Anthropology, Improvisation, and Performance" posted by Brad Fortier on January 12, 2011, at http://bradfortier.com/2011/01/12/on-the-road-to-a-new-ethnography-anthropology-improvisation-and-performance/.

3

Forming the Fence: Research Design and Method Review

Though this be madness, yet there is method in't.[1]

HAVING GIVEN THE READER a general sense of the research context and my particular theoretical framework for this study, my discussion in this chapter is focused on describing how the research process unfolded. I detail my research schedule, defend the rationale for my cross-case research design, and explain my sample selection of churches. I then evaluate my over-arching ethnographic methods of participant observation and interviews, and describe summative content analysis, a method specific to my context research (Phase II).

This research is an applied diachronic cross-case study in which I explored the impact of contextual worship arts on the development of church ministry and mission in twelve evangelical churches in and around the city of Beira, Mozambique. Data collection occurred over the course of two years of fieldwork, from 2012 to 2014, and proceeded in four discrete research phases, each with accompanying methods best suited to address the research questions at hand. Triangulation was achieved during the course of the research through the use of multiple methods and data sources. The Research Schedule given in Appendix A

---

1. Shakespeare, *Hamlet*, act 2, scene 2, 193–206.

demonstrates the focus, time-frame, methods used, and data collected in each research phase.[2]

As demonstrated in the Research Schedule, Phase I (September 2012–April 2013) focused on exploring the general research context. I sought to answer the question, "What are Mozambican cultural values of music and the arts, and how are these expressed (both historically and presently) in ministry and missions?" A literary review of Mozambique's history and missional influence and its impact on current worship praxis was my primary method (results detailed in chapter 1). As the literature available was meagre, I also gathered information from "living libraries," older pastors who shared their stories with me about denominational history. These interviews not only provided information but also developed a relationship of mutual trust and respect that proved to be invaluable in the following research phases (information gleaned from these interviews is available in Appendix B, Case Summaries). Participant observation at my primary case site, Família Vitoriosa (VFC), augmented the data gleaned.

Phase II of the research (September 2013–December 2013) delved deeper into the specific urban church context of Beira (see chapters 4 and 5). In this phase, I broadened my research to include twelve cases for a comparative analysis, seeking to answer the research question, "What is the present state of the local church context particularly evidenced in worship praxis?" Methods used included participant observation of worship services at each case site (including performance ethnography at my primary case site), structured and semi-structured interviews with pastors and musicians, and summative content analysis of frequently sung songs.

In Phase III (January 2014–August 2014) I initiated adaptive change through worship praxis. I strove to answer the question, "How can adaptive change in worship praxis be contextualized in order to 'reframe' songwriting workshops in ways that reflect Mozambican cultural values of music and arts and emerging interests of churches, pastors, and worship leaders?" My goal was to expand the songwriting workshop model and, in so doing, to enhance the production of culturally appropriate worship. As this phase involved experimental applied research, methods were conceived based on baseline data collected in research Phase II and

---

2. In an effort to ensure both reliability and validity, the research corpus in its entirety was saved in Dropbox, accessible to research assistants and partners throughout the research project.

adaptive change methodology developed by Heifetz, Grashow, and Linsky (see chapter 6).[3] Employing a multiple baseline design, I introduced factors of the independent variable (adaptive change through contextualized worship arts) to each church over a period of three months. These factors included focus group interviews with pastors and worship leaders at each case site, training opportunities in holding environments to develop a communal core of change (vocal technique classes, jam sessions, and a worship leader's small group), and monthly composer's clubs, a common applied ethnodoxology method.[4] Participant observation (including performance ethnography) continued throughout this third phase.

Finally, Phase IV (September 2014–October 2014) assessed the results of the applied research implemented in Phase III (chapter 7). In this phase I wanted to know what, if any, were the results of changed worship praxis on discipleship within and beyond the local church in Beira? Did the use of contextualized worship arts influence the development of ministry and mission in the participating cases? What were the results of the expanded songwriting workshop model? My methods for this last phase of research included interviews, a self-administered questionnaire, and continued participant observation.

Now that the reader has a general sense of the four research phases and their accompanying methods and data collected, I move to defend the rationale for the cross-case research design and my sample selection, to analyze the overarching methods of participant observation and interviews used throughout the study, and to describe summative content analysis, a method used exclusively in Phase II.

FRAMING THE FENCE: RESEARCH DESIGN

Every researcher has underlying interpretive frameworks, whether clearly articulated or not, that guide their research process. By the end of the initial research phase (Phase I) I had a clear sense of the philosophical assumptions, paradigms, and theories that would situate this qualitative research project.[5] I conducted this research from a critical theory perspective, allowing me to acknowledge my own power and position as a white female missionary within the study through reflexivity, and

---

3. Heifetz, Grashow, and Linsky, *Practice of Adaptive Leadership*.

4. King, *Pathways in Christian Music*.

5. Three paradigms correlate with these philosophical assumptions, social constructivism, participatory action research (PAR), and pragmatism.

to minimize objective separateness between myself and the research participants. I engaged in dialogues with pastors and worship leaders with the intention of encouraging participants themselves to transform their current worship praxis. Method discovery was an inductive process, emerging *in situ* as I collected and analyzed the data. This methodological stance, therefore, directed which research design I chose.

Cross-Case Study Research Design

Having determined my basic interpretive framework, I needed to select a qualitative inquiry approach that would best answer my research questions. I wanted to understand how the contemporary phenomenon of contextual worship arts impacted "clearly identifiable cases" (urban church contexts in Beira) over a defined period of time.[6] Thus, a cross-case study approach allowed me to compare and contrast how contextualized worship praxis shaped ministry and mission in the various church communities.

As case studies can sometimes become less rigorous, by not following systematic procedures and allowing biases to influence findings, it was essential that I employ strategies to combat these tendencies. One means of strengthening the study was to expand it to a cross-case study. Yin makes a compelling argument for multiple-case studies when he reasons that "when you have the choice (and resources), multiple-case designs may be preferred over single-case designs. Single-case designs are vulnerable if only because you will have put all your eggs in one basket."[7] Other techniques I used to reinforce the study included following systematic procedures through the use of a case-study protocol, and triangulating methods and data sources to diminish "fishing tendencies."[8]

Expanding the study, while making the evidence more robust, was not just a matter of picking more churches at random. In fact, Yin argues that each case in a cross-case study, "should serve a specific purpose within the overall scope of inquiry ... that is, to follow a replication logic" rather than a sampling logic.[9] To this end, a brief synopsis of the purpose of each case is in order here. How did I expand from my primary case,

---

6. Creswell, *Qualitative Inquiry*, 74.

7. Yin, *Case Study Research*, 53.

8. "Fishing tendencies" refers to the potential to corrupt findings by seeing specific answers to the exclusion of other data.

9. Yin, *Case Study Research*, 47.

Família Vitoriosa (VFC), to a cross-case study, and how did I choose the other eleven churches?

Sample Selection

Having had prior exposure to worship praxis at Família Vitoriosa (VFC), I was interested in discovering if my experiences were isolated to this case, or were evidence of a more broad-based phenomenon. I was therefore interested in gathering a variety of perspectives, and my samples needed to reflect this diversity. I was also concerned about promoting adaptive change; I needed to not only gather a diverse representation of evangelical churches, but also to partner with influential churches that could, in turn, disseminate change to other churches.

Maura Juça Manuel, a missionary in Beira for over twenty years, suggested an additional eight churches[10] as a representative sample of the most influential churches in Beira. Having limited time with which to sift through the hundreds of options, I relied on Maura's historical knowledge of the urban church context. She has taught for many years at Instituto Bíblico de Sofala (IBS), a local seminary, and while in contact with a multitude of pastors and denominations, is not formally affiliated with one. In fact, the church that she is partnering with was not included in this study. Therefore, I felt that Maura's suggestions would not unduly compensate or give an unfair advantage to a particular church or denomination.

The last three cases were selected as follows. Pastor João of Família Vitoriosa (VFC), my primary case site, recommended American Board (AB); the pastors of Missão Evangélica Vida Nova (MEVN) and Aurora Messiânica (AM) approached me, asking to participate in the research. Aside from AB, these last two cases are newer church plants, having been established in the last 10–15 years. They (along with VFC, another younger church) provided a counterpoint to AB and the eight cases recommended by Maura (all with an established history in Beira for at least thirty years).

While the cases shared a common location (Beira) and could be grouped under the general category of evangelical, they represented diverse cases. The findings reflected the differences but also revealed generalized similarities. This comparative approach promoted depth and

---

10. UB, VPD, NA, ECD, ADA, ADI, ADE and 1stB—see Abbreviations for full church names.

complexity and helped me better understand the phenomenon (effect of contextualized worship arts) shared among diverse cases (urban churches in Beira), building external validity through replication logic.

Though twelve cases was a large number of churches to compare, it proved to be a necessary amount, as I encountered significant difficulties in garnering full participation from each case. Having a broader base of cases gave me some wiggle room without forfeiting data saturation. Only four churches participated fully in each research phase (see conclusion for a more detailed discussion). As the research progressed, these four diverse cases helped me develop a theoretical framework that stated the conditions under which certain worship praxis was likely to be found (literal replication), as well as the conditions for which it was not likely to be found (theoretical replication).[11] The remaining eight cases, then, provided compelling support for my initial propositions about contextualized worship praxis.

GETTING THE GOATS: METHOD REVIEW

In the following section, I describe my reasoning for the primary methods used in all of the research phases, participant observation, and interviews, and how these methods helped to answer my research questions. I then delve into the methodology specific to the second phase of this study, summative content analysis. Chapter 6 investigates the adaptive change experimental methods specific to the third phase of research, structured interviews in focus groups, and experimental interventions in holding environments (including composer's clubs). Chapter 7 describes the method specific to the fourth phase of research, a self-administered questionnaire.

Participant Observation through Performance Ethnography

Participant observation is a strategic method that "puts you where the action is and lets you collect data."[12] Though it is one of the most ethically problematic of research methods due to its manipulative tendencies, I would not have been able to adequately address my research questions without it. Participant observation gave me access to music events as not just an observer but also as a performer. My regular presence at

---

11. Yin, *Case Study Research*, 47–48.
12. Bernard, *Social Research Methods*, 318.

music events built trust, which lowered participant's reactivity, helped me formulate sensible questions *in situ*, and clarified the meaning of the data. As an active investigator, I was able to engineer meetings and events, a key component of the third phase of research in which I was applying adaptive change.

The major problem with this method, namely resultant biases towards supporting the cases being studied, was recognized from the beginning. Congruent with my philosophical research stance, I unashamedly wanted to advocate for the churches being studied. The challenge was not in engaging the research context, for as a missionary practitioner that is exactly what I wanted to do, but in seeing the results through "rose-colored glasses." How did I compensate for the real temptation to discover positive change through contextualized worship arts that did not exist or was not as positive as I would have hoped?

Though it is unlikely one can ever be completely separated from one's biases, I believe solid scientific research demands that the researcher acknowledge their values they bring to the study, broaden the study to include cases that may disprove emerging propositions, carefully follow research protocol, develop a chain of evidence with a case study database, and allow key informants to review the report drafts. These measures that I used, while certainly not fool-proof, diminished the likelihood of unreasonable bias, and built greater validity and reliability.

Performance ethnography, working as a musician in partnership with other musicians to make music, is a particular means of participant observation frequently used in ethnomusicology. It engenders a more reflexive means of participant observation, allowing the researcher to understand the music event from an "emic" perspective.[13] Kisliuk is perhaps one of the most well-known ethnomusicologists who effectively used performance ethnography in her research among the BaAka in the Central African Republic. She advocates a dramatic shift toward reflexive, non-objectivist scholarship, stating, "When we begin to participate in music and dance our very being merges with the 'field' through our bodies and voices, and another Self-Other boundary is dissolved."[14]

This methodology allowed me to participate in worship rehearsals, dance with congregants in celebration during offertory, play piano at weddings, and learn to play the *mbira* (thumb piano). In so doing, I

13. Berliner, *Soul of Mbira*; Chitando, *Singing Culture*; Steingo, "After Apartheid"; Higashi, "Musical Communitas."

14. Kisliuk, "(Un)Doing Fieldwork," 183.

gained a better understanding of the music culture from the inside, experiencing the behind-the-scenes social dynamics and the challenges of performance on a personal level.

I supplemented my subjective experiences in performance ethnography with field notes, journaling, and audiovisual materials, largely video recordings, still photos, and digital audio recordings.[15] At church services, I used a simple event observation report to guide my observational process, focusing on artifacts, actors, and activities (see Appendix C for a sample observation report). Video clips were later compiled into 5–7 minute sample videos used in focus groups at each church in Phase III (see chapter 6).

Using accompanying data addresses another weakness of participant observation (particularly performance ethnography), that participation in the event may require too much attention relative to observation of the event. These additional materials enhanced my analysis in that they allowed me to capture a different point of view, and to repeatedly review the event to catch components I may have missed in my preliminary observations and notes, a form of triangulation within the method itself.

The data analysis process for the participant observation field notes was fairly straightforward. After ensuring that all the field notes were uploaded to my computer, I printed them out, grouped them into categories, and sorted by date. I then performed a thematic analysis of each data set; building internal validity by looking specifically for the answers to my sub-problems (explanation building), commonalities between the various cases (pattern matching), and practices unique to each case (addressing rival explanations).

Interviews

Interviews, along with participant observation, are the "bread and butter" of ethnographic fieldwork. Qualitative interviewing takes the researcher's observations a step further; it is a means of discovering what others feel and think about their worlds. In my research context, interviews were a critical component, as many events were in languages other than Portuguese. In order to understand what was happening I had to ask questions such as, "What do the words of this song mean?"

Informal interviewing, therefore, flowed naturally from participant observation. I constantly asked clarifying questions about what I

---

15. Chitando, *Singing Culture*; Tan, "Transformative Worship."

was observing, or I used the opportunities afforded by social events to ask more probing questions about an interaction or to describe historic details, the event itself triggered my questions and the answers. I dealt with the pitfall of bias due to interpersonal influence in the interviews by relying on multiple informants and corroborating insights with other sources of information gleaned from participant observation.

Semi-structured interviews, conducted in Phase I, were a great entrée into a relationship with a pastor and his church. Although most of these interviews were initially with pastors I had not met, these types of interviews felt most natural in that they allowed for flexibility of question and response. Though I had an interview guide (I wanted to know about their personal and church history), I maintained discretion to follow leads the conversation presented. These interviews helped me develop rapport with pastors, gaining access to worship services and music events in churches; a vital component of Phase I of the research.

Validity was built by having informants familiar with Beira church history review the case summaries (Appendix B), the cumulative results of these interviews. This proved to be an important step, as I found that some of my case data was incorrect. It is likely that I misunderstood the pastors, due to my faulty Portuguese ability. I did not bring a digital recorder to these initial interviews, so I only had my notes I took during the meetings from which to create the summaries. Other hindrances to accuracy could have included a pastor's faulty memory, or his desire to make a favorable impression on a missionary. Unfortunately, as the history of much of these churches has not been published, and there are very few pastors who know about early denominational history, it is incredibly difficult to verify the pastors' stories.

I attempted a semi-structured interview with a modified focus group of Baptist pastors at a convention. While I hoped they would have similar responses and would have a sense of camaraderie due to denominational ties, I found the interview to be one of the more difficult. I suspect that this was due, in part, to some participants' opportunistic motivations (confirmed by my research partner) and, in part, to other pastors' hesitations to be vulnerable in front of their peers, exacerbated by my direct questions. Saving face and nonconfrontational cultural values affected the quality of the interview. It became clear when dealing with pastors that one-on-one interviews were less intimidating and yielded better responses. However, focus groups at each site with the pastor, church leadership, and worship leaders in the third phase of research proved to be a pivotal component of initiating adaptive change in that it engaged leaders in the change process (see chapter 6).

I conducted face-to-face structured interviews with pastors in Phase II and Phase IV. These interviews were more restrictive than the semi-structured interviews in that I followed an interview schedule. My questioning route for Phase II, though pilot tested, did not yield data that was directly relevant to my research questions (see Appendix E for questioning route and compiled responses). However, by Phase IV, the questions and responses yielded rich data for analysis, providing crucial evidence for the data assessment.

Bernard states that "personal interviews are costly in both time and money,"[16] a disadvantage to this interviewing approach. While I concur, the time and money invested not only produced convergent themes, complementing the reality witnessed in participant observation at each site, but also continued to build relational capital. In the case of the structured interviews, it was not so much the information gleaned during the interviews, but the relationships built as a result of these interviews that was well worth the cost.

Many Beira pastors are bi-vocational, and few have offices or office hours. This reality can make it difficult to make and keep an appointment with a pastor. Therefore, when I was able to meet with a pastor in phase II, I also used the interview appointment as a time to explain the research and to formalize the research relationship (through a consent form). Conforming to case study protocol, this signed consent form allowed me access to interviews, church services, and training opportunities with worship leaders and church members. Having learned my lesson about the importance of secondary sources of evidence to validate accuracy from my semi-structured interviews, I digitally recorded each structured interview and took notes, which I then used to create summary transcriptions.

Summative Content Analysis

Aside from participant observations and interviews, I used collections of frequently sung songs as the third source of data to study the present state of the Beira church context evidenced through worship praxis (Phase II). King suggests content analysis of song lyrics as a technique for discovering a church's "lyric theology," that is, what the church understands and

---

16. Bernard, *Social Research Methods*, 231.

knows about God through song.[17] An analysis of song lyrics from various churches revealed underlying beliefs pointing to spiritual weaknesses and strengths, and areas of growth for church ministry and mission.

This final method of Phase II proved to be invaluable. Though I could witness subject's levels of participation and emotional engagement during church services, I rarely knew what they were singing about (unless I found someone who could translate for me), as the majority of songs were not in Portuguese. Therefore, I was missing the meaning of the songs sung. Summative content analysis, "a group collaborative analytic technique that concentrates on consensus-building activities,"[18] was a method that reached past my language limitations and researcher bias. Song lyrics were an exact data source with broad coverage that extended beyond my observations during a singular worship event.

The challenge at the outset in using this method was to create a protocol that could satisfy the rigors of qualitative research and be locally applied. I gathered a cluster sample of frequently sung songs from nine various churches for a total of 154 songs. My sampling plan was achieved by asking the pastor or a worship leader to give me the words to twenty frequently sung songs from their church. Sometimes the songs collected were simply the songs that had been sung recently at a service, sometimes they were the first twenty that came to the worship leader's mind, or were, perhaps, their favorites.

As Beira evangelical churches generally sing around five congregational songs per week (with little seasonal or liturgical variation), twenty songs represented a month's worth of congregational songs, and was a reasonable sample size per church from which to generalize. In most cases it was labor-intensive to collect a complete sample of twenty, as people had to remember and recite them to me line-by-line (often singing to remember the words). I was not able to collect a sample from three participating churches (ADA, ADE, and AB), and my samples from AM (three songs) and ECD (eleven songs) were incomplete.[19]

Some songs were in Portuguese, some in English, Ndau, Sena, and even Shona.[20] When not in Portuguese, the songs were also translated into Portuguese so that there was a common language for analysis (nine-

---

17. King, *Music in the Life*, 35.
18. Rapport, "Summative Analysis," 270.
19. See Abbreviations.
20. Ndau, Sena, and Shona are languages commonly spoken in central Mozambique.

ty-one songs were originally in vernacular, sixty-two were in Portuguese, one was in English). I recruited two young Christian worship leaders, with music degrees from Eduardo Mondlane University in Maputo, to be my research assistants.[21]

After explaining the summative content analysis methodology, and having them sign a research agreement form, we did blind testing on each cluster sample. We filled in the protocol table and ranked the songs like a stop light (green = good biblical content, yellow = use with caution/make some changes, red = unbiblical/confusing), then compared notes to check for inter-coder reliability. We built consensus on the song ranking and our suggestions for future use of these songs in each church. I then took the results of the analysis back to select pastors for additional validity checks, asking the following questions: Do our results match up with the reality in your church? What's missing according to you when you look at the results? What other spiritual needs are present? Their answers were fodder for focus group discussions, songwriting workshops, and training foci in Phase III.

SUMMARY

In this chapter I detailed my research schedule and discussed the rationale behind a cross-case research design. I reviewed my over-arching methods of participant observation through performance ethnography and interviews. I also described summative content analysis, a method specific to the second phase of this research. These research pieces formed the "fence" for this particular study. Though I was an active researcher, intentionally engaging in the context, I adjusted for bias and built validity and reliability into the study design, developing converging lines of inquiry through triangulation of methods and data sources. I now move to a presentation and analysis of my Phase II findings that demonstrate the lack of teaching and practice of contextualized worship arts in the development of disciples in Beira churches.

---

21. Eduardo Mondlane University in Maputo (the capital of Mozambique) is currently the only accredited music degree program in the country. These young men received a small monetary remuneration for their work as detailed by the research agreement form that they signed.

PART TWO

The Pasture: Discovering Present State of Church Contexts

IN PART ONE, I situated the research by describing the landscape of this study, the unique features of multicultural urban migration, and distinctive elements of mission influence that have shaped worship praxis in Mozambican evangelical churches in Beira. I detailed my guiding theoretical framework, demonstrating how both the disciplines of ethnomusicology and missiology have historically failed to address worship music as a subject of analysis and as a tool for ministry. Finally, I described my research process, illustrating how I conducted this study that sits at the crossroads between urban ethnomusicology and applied missiology.

Having given the reader a picture of the general context in which Beira churches reside, and the location and frame of this study, in Part II (The Pasture) I reveal my findings and analysis. In chapter 4, "Gathering the Goats: What Does Worship Look Like in Beira?" I describe current worship praxis, while in chapter 5, "Vetting the Herd: Data Analysis," I reveal a lack of teaching and practice of contextualized worship arts in the development of disciples in Beira churches.

4

Gathering the Goats: What Does Worship Look Like in Beira?

> *Abre as comportas do céu, faz chover, faz chover....*[1] With hands raised and voices united we sang to God, begging him to open the floodgates of heaven and let it rain, let it rain to relieve us of the oppressive humidity and the increasingly corrupt and chaotic political system whose attacks the day prior during an election campaign in the city of Beira left three dead and many wounded.
>
> It was as if we were pleading along with the prophet Amos, "Let justice roll on like a river, righteousness like a never-failing stream!" Thirsting for peace, we cried out in hopeful worship to God, believing that only He could answer our prayers.[2]

THE MEDIUM OF THE written word seems a poor tool for describing a multi-layered sensory ritual experience that is a typical worship service in Beira. Arranged letters cannot adequately capture the sound of hearts raised in praise, or the movement of joyful feet celebrating through offering, or the feeling of community that comes from worshipping with others. Yet I am tasked with the impossible here, providing an ethno-

---

1. "Open the floodgates of heaven, let it rain, let it rain." lyrics from Michael W. Smith, "Let it Rain," 2008.

2. Meyers, Assembleia de Deus Evangélica (ADE) site visit, field notes, 2013–14.

graphic "thick description"[3] of worship in Beira through my fieldwork experiences from 2012–14.

To add to my challenge, I have twelve churches to describe, in a limited amount of space, without taxing my reader. Yin suggests, in cross-case studies like mine, to present a general description and appending detailed case studies.[4] So, I begin this chapter with a cross-case comparison of the twelve churches, noting commonalities and differences. This will give the reader a quick snapshot of the diverse research context. However, as demographics are just a starting point, I will then delve deeper into the music culture of worship in Beira as practiced during Sunday church services. The total research corpus for Phase II, gathered from September to December of 2013 is as follows:

1. Participant observation: 6 church services, 9 site visits, 4 music events, 20 rehearsals/meetings, 2 composer's clubs (pilot tests), 7 IBS classes
2. Interviews: 10 structured interviews with pastors
3. Summative content analysis: 154 songs (9 churches)

Anthony Seeger defines an ethnography of music as "a descriptive approach to music going beyond the writing down of sounds to the writing down of how songs are conceived, made, appreciated, and influence other individuals, groups, and social and musical processes."[5] This intimates that this chapter must detail not only the music itself, but it must also describe the surrounding social environment in which music is played.

James Spradley states, "Every social situation can be identified by three primary elements: a place, actors, and activities."[6] Lingenfelter adds two additional elements saying, "The features of any social environment include the following: space, people, relationships, activities, and time."[7] Artifacts (particularly in a church service) are another key factor.

---

3. The term "thick description" was used by Clifford Geertz in his book *The Interpretation of Cultures* to describe his ethnographic method (5–6, 9–10).

4. Yin, *Case Study Research*, 54. See Appendix B for case summaries.

5. Seeger, "Ethnography of Music," 89.

6. Spradley, *Participant Observation*, 39.

7. Lingenfelter, *Agents of Transformation*, 35.

Gathering the Goats: What Does Worship Look Like in Beira?

Jeff Titon's music-performance model[8] best addresses both the social and the musical components that create the music event of worship in Beira churches. Using Titon's model as a rubric, then, I describe the four domains of Beira's worship music performance in the last half of the chapter, illustrating the time and space, audience and community, performers and performance, and the music and its affective experience.

GENERALIZATIONS ABOUT BEIRA CHURCHES

> Religion is an integral part of Mozambican societal life. All communities in Mozambique profess belief in the existence of a supreme being.[9]

According to census results, Christians make up just over half of the Mozambican population.[10] I limited my research to twelve evangelical churches (excluding Catholics and other variants considered syncretistic by Mozambicans). The twelve churches researched, therefore, represent just a slice of the total Christian worshipping population in Beira. In Table 2, I offer a snapshot of the church demographics, giving the reader a general sense of the types of churches researched, including the missional influence, the approximate year of inception, congregational size and ethnicity, language used, music style, and instruments used in worship. Further descriptions of the music styles and instruments follow in the repertories of music section.

Of the churches visited, 75 percent are Pentecostal in a broad sense, demonstrating freedom of charismatic expression in worship. Though all the Western-initiated churches (WIC) could now be considered indigenous churches in that they are self-sustaining, self-governing, and self-propagating, half still demonstrate strong connections with their foreign mission legacy in their worship praxis.[11] Família Vitoriosa (VFC), Evangelho Completo de Deus (ECD), and Assembleia de Deus Evangêlica (ADE), however, practice forms of worship (to varying degrees) that

---

8. Titon, *Worlds of Music*, 11.

9. Ndege, *Culture and Customs*, 21.

10. A census taken by the National Institute of Statistics in 2007 reported that 56.1 percent of Mozambicans were Christian, 17.9 percent Muslim (primarily Sunni), 18.7 percent no religion, and 7.3 percent other ("Religion in Mozambique," Wikipedia, http://en.wikipedia.org/wiki/Religion-in-Mozambique).

11. Venn and Anderson, Shanghai Conference, 1892. See p. 5, n. 10.

more closely reflect local cultural norms.[12] In the case of VFC, this is due, in part, to the founding missionaries themselves. They were non-Western (from Singapore and Brazil) and belonged to a newer generation of missionaries who embraced contextualization as a missional value.

Table 2: Beira Church Demographics

Church Name	Missional Influence	Date	Size	Ethnicity	Language Used	Music Style	Instruments (wstrn/trad)
VFC	WIC	1998	~200	Mix	Portuguese	NM/PS	W
1stB	WIC	1979	~400	Mix	Portuguese	WH/NM/PS	W/T
VPD	AIC	1948	~100	Ndau	Ndau/Port	WH/NM/PS	W
UB	WIC	1920s	~100	Lomwe	Lomwe/Port	WH/NM	W
NA	AIC	1920s	~100	Sena	Sena/Port	WH/NM	W
ECD	WIC	1928	~100	Ndau	Ndau/Port	WH/NM	W
ADA	AIC	1920s	~100	Mix	Shona/Port	NM/PS	W
ADI	AIC	1950s	~200	Mix	Sena/Port	NM/PS	W
ADE	WIC	1920s	~300	Mix	Portuguese	WH/NM/PS	W
MEVN	AIC	2005	~200	Mix	Portuguese	NM/PS	W
AM	AIC	2004	~50	Mix	Port/Makua	WH/NM/PS	W/T
AB	WIC	1930s	~200	Ndau	Ndau/Port	WH/NM/PS	T

Key: AIC: African-Initiated Churches; WIC: Western-initiated Churches; NM: *Nossa Música*; PS: Portuguese Songs; WH: Western Hymns; W: Western instruments; T: Traditional instruments

Of the six African-initiated churches (AIC), historic connections to WICs can be traced for at least three. "Many AIC Christians and their leaders were one-time members of Western mission churches but eventually chose to part ways or were expelled for precisely this reason."[13] This is certainly true in the case of Nova Aliança (NA) (once associated with the Plymouth Brethren) and even could be argued to be valid to a lesser degree for Assembleia de Deus Internaçional (ADI) and Visão na Palavra de Deus (VPD) (with initial links to Apostles of Faith

---

12. One example of this acculturation is the abandonment of the use of hymnals.
13. King, *Music in the Life*, 68.

Gathering the Goats: What Does Worship Look Like in Beira?

Mission and Zionist churches respectively). Aurora Messiânica (AM) and Missão Evangêlica da Vida Nova (MEVN), however, are younger church plants founded by Mozambican pastors directly after they finished their seminary training.

Though the congregational size of these local churches is relatively small, four have churches in all ten of Mozambique's provinces; all (save one) have planted daughter churches and have multiple parishes throughout the city. Seven churches reach a mixed ethnic population, necessitating the use of Portuguese for worship; five churches are ethnic churches. In these cases, services are conducted in both mother tongue and Portuguese.

Languages used in services can indicate the ethnicity of the founding pastor (as in the case of Aurora Messiânica) or the location of the founding church. Assembleia de Deus Africana (ADA) was founded in Zimbabwe, so services are still conducted in both Shona and Portuguese. União Baptista (UB) was originally founded among the Lomwe of the Zambezi Valley. As they migrated to the city, they brought their denomination and their ethnic ties with them.

All churches use a variety of music styles. All Western-initiated churches (WIC) use Western hymns (showing clear missional influence), while Portuguese songs are more common in the younger churches (established post-independence). This correlates with the wave of Evangelical mission efforts in Mozambique in the early 1990s. *Nossa música* (our music) is a ubiquitous indigenous style across denominational lines.

Only one church in twelve cases used traditional instruments exclusively (AB). However, this was situational on the Sunday I visited, and AB is not opposed to using Western instruments. Another church (UB) is adverse to traditional instruments, citing missionary counsel as the primary basis. Ninety-two percent of the churches studied used Western instruments.

The evidence clearly shows that the cases studied exhibit healthy congregational growth (in terms of numbers) and strong missional inclinations (numerous church plants) despite the challenges, in seven cases, of a multiethnic urban congregation. Foreign mission influence and globalization trends, however, are substantiated in the song style and instruments used during services. Though worship was heartfelt, there was a palpable performative difference across the music styles, and led me to wonder how much greater the growth would be if the churches could wholeheartedly adopt a contextualized worship arts model for ministry and missions.

MUSIC-CULTURE PERFORMANCE MODEL APPLIED TO BEIRA CHURCHES

> A music-culture ultimately rests in the people themselves—their ideas, their actions, and the sound they produce.[14]

Having painted broad brushstrokes outlining general characteristics of churches and their worship styles, a description of the finer details of Mozambican music-culture in Christian worship is now in order. Titon defines a music-culture as "a group's total involvement with music: ideas, actions, institutions, material objects, everything that has to do with music."[15] What is the music-culture of worship in Beira churches? What do *Beirenses* think about music, what do they do when they make music, what kinds of music do they use to worship, and what instruments are used? I answer these questions using Titon's music-culture model that is grounded in music as it is performed (see figure 3). This model starts with the music at the center, and the affective experience on those involved in the event. It radiates out to include the performers and their performance as it moves along prescribed rules and procedures, and then the surrounding audience and community that carries on the norms and traditions of performance. Finally, the event is situated in a time and space, the contextual setting in which a music event occurs.

---

14. Merriman, *Anthropology of Music*, 32–33.
15. Titon, *Worlds of Music*, 4.

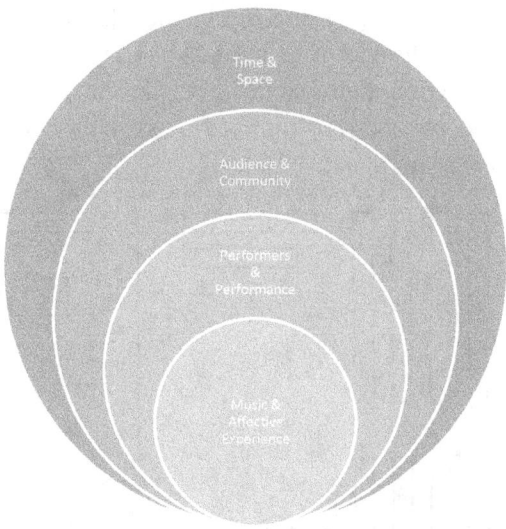

Figure 3: Elements of a Music Performance

Rather than start in the center, however, I will start at the periphery, working my way from the outside in, as this best illustrates the way one experiences a worship music event in Beira churches. First, one approaches the setting, in this case, a church building in which the music event occurs. As one enters the building, one joins a community of faith gathered to worship. The service begins with performers following ascribed patterns of behavior in relation to each other and to the music, which, in turn, is meaningfully organized sound that produces emotional impact. This portrayal will provide the reader with a magnified lens through which to view the reality of worship as performed in Beira churches today.

Time and Space

Though I attended services that represented a wide array of denominational proclivities, each church building (from an old cement block and tin roof structure in a shanty town to a modern rented conference room in a high-rise building in the city center) is rectangular in shape. Each has a center aisle (in some cases, two aisles), with benches or chairs facing a raised front platform or altar with a pulpit. Figure 4 is a map of Visão na Palavra de Deus (VPD), demonstrating a typical church layout and design.

Creature comforts are a rare commodity. Though some churches have fans to blow the heavy hot air around, there is no other means of climate control, aside from personal fans or cloths that people bring. Seats are hard, some people sit on *esteiras* (reed mats) on the floor, while others stand when there is no room.

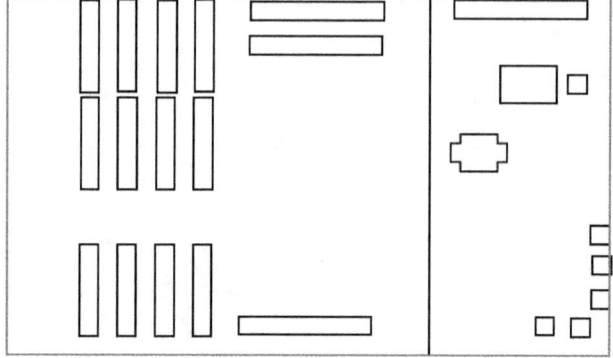

Figure 4: Church Layout

Though the churches are regularly cleaned (I generally arrive early enough to see someone dusting off furniture or sweeping the floor), and many have some sort of décor (plants, paper chains hung from the ceiling, curtains, scripture verses painted on the walls, clocks, most of which don't work, altar coverings, offering baskets), practical use of the space, rather than aesthetic sensibility seems to be a governing principle. It is not uncommon to see a motorbike, cooking utensils, or construction materials also stored in a corner of the sanctuary.[16]

---

16. Scott, in her book *Moving into African Music* explains, "In Africa, material things are to be used, not treated like treasures unless related to a belief system, and our western insistence on order and cleanliness is felt to border on idolatry," 23.

Gathering the Goats: What Does Worship Look Like in Beira?

Figure 5: Sanctuary

Aesthetic value in personal dress, however, is important. People generally dress their best, from suit coats and ties (even on the hottest days) to fancy dress and head wraps, showing that a church service is a special time, different from daily activities. Women's wear is conservative, similar to the surrounding cultural context. If a woman is wearing pants, she may put on a *capulana* (wrap), especially before going forward to give an offering or to sing up front. Women also use *capulanas* to cover their knees if their skirts are short enough to show their knees when seated. Sleeveless tops are sometimes covered with additional shirts or shawls. In many churches women wear *lenços* (hankies or head wraps) to cover their hair.

Audience and Community

Seating arrangements are important and indicate rank and responsibility. Pastors, leaders, and honored guests have seats at the front of the sanctuary, some on the platform itself. The most respected people literally have the best seats in the house. *Jovens* (youth) also have a seating area, often in the choir "loft." Moms with young children may sit on *esteiras* (reed mats) at the back of the sanctuary, allowing for privacy while feeding and flexibility to come and go as needed with fussy babies. Some churches now offer some form of *Escola Dominical* (Sunday School) for children, which may take place before, during, or after the service (sometimes in the sanctuary or outside under the shade of a mango tree).

Aside from the pastor whose main responsibility during a Sunday service is preaching, there are a few other key actors. The master of ceremonies (MC), or *dirigente do culto*, guides the order of service, welcoming visitors, announcing what comes next in the program, and asking members to testify or to lead in song. The MC is the closest functional equivalent to the Western concept of "worship leader."

Other roles include a secretary (who gives the announcements), a treasurer (who guides the offertory process), a translator, and a choir master (who leads special choral presentations). Recently, some churches have added a *grupo do louvor* (praise group), mostly comprised of youth, who will lead congregational singing. These groups sometimes have a lead singer. These roles can be interchangeable (the secretary is the MC, or the lead singer also translates for the pastor). While these leadership roles are clearly defined, there is regular congregational participation, from testimonies, to prayers, to congregational leading of songs.

Performers and Performance

A strong event orientation is evident in how and when services start. I would arrive at the churches at the time the pastors indicated the services started, and usually kept company with mosquitoes and perhaps someone cleaning the sanctuary. One pastor, with whom I've had conversations about time and cultural differences in punctuality, said to me (after waiting for a half hour past the stated start time of the service), "Now you know what Mozambican time is like!"[17] People generally drift in slowly, and then some songs start (often led by seated congregants), or people begin to pray, loudly and collectively pouring their hearts out to God. These songs are a signal that the service is starting.

The order of service varies from church to church and is flexible from week to week. Generally, there is an initial time of congregational singing and praying, followed by welcome and announcements and sometimes testimonies, then another *quente* (hot) song or two before the sermon. "The pastor has to preach and pray. Let's sing so that the pastor only has to preach!"[18]

---

17. Meyers, field notes, 2013–14.
18. Meyers, field notes, 2012–13.

This quote by an MC indicates a general sentiment that there is a marked difference between the singing and praying time and the sermon. "We've left the worship time now . . . the first part is the time when you arrive early and pray, praise and worship. The second part is the preaching part."[19] Preaching is not necessarily considered part of worship.

Music mediates the majority of the church service; from calling people to worship, to filling space in between various activities, or as an underlying support during prayers and testimonies. The only time music is not used during a service, although some pastors sing songs to emphasize a sermon point, is during the preaching. Save for select presentations (and even then it is common for members to sing, shout, or dance along), music is highly participatory, involving the entire congregation and the whole body. As Roberta King often states in class, "We don't just worship from the neck up!" Even in the more conservative churches, movement of some sort (clapping, swaying, stepping) was part of the music.

Many worship leaders, pastors, and students asked me to clarify the difference between "praise" and "worship."[20] Though I was not able to discover how this worship philosophy arrived in Beira, it has resulted in a belief that *tempo* is the distinguishing characteristic between "praise" and "worship." My research experiences revealed service orders that generally flowed from active, gathering praise songs to more reflective worship songs before the sermon. However, this was not a consistent phenomenon and varied from denomination to denomination.

---

19. Meyers, field notes, 2013–14.

20. This differentiation arose from Pentecostal liturgical ideology based on temple imagery in Ps 100, in which a service begins with "praise" (upbeat congregational songs), then moves to a time of "worship" (slower songs for individual reflection and reverence). See Matthew Sigler's article, "Misplacing Charisma."

Figure 6: Offering

Though communion in the evangelical church community is generally celebrated once a month, offerings are a weekly affair. Sometimes differentiations are made between tithes and offerings, sometimes social groups or parishes are called to give by group ("now the *jovens* will bring their offerings"), sometimes there are altar, general, or mercy offerings. Regardless of the particularities, all offerings are given with a sense of joyful celebration through song and dance. This is another highly participatory part of the church service where traditional Mozambican cultural means of celebration are more evident, spontaneous dancing, ululation, clapping, and throwing money at the offering basket.

Special music presentations by the youth choir, the mothers, and the children's choir are another common element in church services. Most times the groups rhythmically process down the aisle to the front with a song, then present a song, and recess down the aisle with a final song. The congregation will generally cheer the choirs on with clapping, ululation, sometimes shouting, "*Faia!*" (literally fire, or it's hot!), or standing up and joining in singing and dancing. Other service elements include testimonies, greetings, and announcements.

The practice of music-making in worship reflects multiple social norms. Worship music serves societal functions, in this case, community building, and is always multimedia (music and dance). The musical style is improvisational, rarely is there a fixed song set or composition. Rather, the music flows by feel. Strong group values lead to high participation and a blurred distinction between audience and performer. Worship praxis in Beira is participatory (everyone present is doing something), rather than presentational (clear divide between the performers and the audience).[21] There is a sense of group ownership and aptitude; *nossa música*, our music.

Music and Affective Experience, Repertories of Music

Having briefly discussed the surrounding context and the community that produces worship music events in Beira churches, I move to a more detailed analysis of the music itself. In this examination I will use a component model to describe the repertories of worship music in Beira, including the genres and styles, composition and transmission, movement, material culture, and song texts.

Genres and Styles

Scott describes three typical African music styles in her chapter entitled, "A Style Alphabet."[22] A, or home music, is what ethnomusicologists describe as heart music, the sounds people hear from birth that are the traditional music of their home culture. B, or pan-African music, retains style A characteristics (pentatonic scale, cyclic rhythm pattern, polyphonic harmony sung in vernacular) but crosses geographical and urban boundaries, accessible across Africa. C, or foreign music, is characterized by melodic variety.

In Mozambican church music there are also three distinct self-determined genres of worship music: *nossa música*, Portuguese music (Brazilian worship songs, or versions of worship music from the US or Australia translated into Portuguese), and Western hymns. *Nossa música* is type B music, while Portuguese music and Western hymns can be categorized as type C.

Nossa música has a very "African" style, a chord progression using I, IV, and V with a singable melody (often sung in antiphonal phrases),

21. See Turino, *Music as Social Life*.
22. Scott, *Moving Into African Music*, 44–53.

and a danceable polyrhythm (upbeat tempo). The texts are sometimes biblically based, some direct Scripture quotations, and are generally one sentence long; *Mwari wakanaka, iya!* (God is good, yeah!). *Nossa música* is almost always performed with rhythmic movement (clapping, jumping, and swaying).

Portuguese music has two styles. Worship songs from Brazil often have a bossa nova or samba feel (rhythm) to them, with complex chord progressions. The song form is similar to standard Western popular worship songs (verse, chorus, verse, chorus ... bridge). As they were composed in Portuguese by Portuguese speakers, the texts fit well with the melody.

Translated English songs are easily recognizable as the Portuguese translation doesn't always fit well with the melody, the chords used are regularly I, IV, and V, and the rhythm is consistently 4/4. Alterations to the original melody and the rhythm are sometimes made, this may be an intentional move toward acculturation, or simply distortion due to distance from the original context and an inability to play the song as originally intended.

Western hymns are sung in Western-initiated churches (WICs), or in churches that still maintain a strong connection to their missionary heritage. Most hymnals do not include a music score (though some have tonic sol-fa notation), they are simply translated texts into Portuguese or other local languages, sometimes profoundly deviating from the original lyrics or tune.[23] Musical adaptation is evident in how the hymns are sung. Vocal leading and filler between stanzas gives a call and response feel to even the most foreign of church music styles.

Song Texts

All church songs, regardless of the genre, have words. This means that they use two communication systems, language and music, necessitating an exploration of both.[24] I conducted summative content analysis on 154 songs texts from nine different churches. Of the total number of songs,

---

23. The Portuguese lyrics to the melody of "O Come All Ye Faithful" are as follows, "*Louvamos, louvamos Senhor e adoramos/A ti oh Deus Homem no çeu asentado/Que em tempo de vida na terra humilhado/Por nossos pecados, morrestes na cruz*" (We praise and worship you Lord/To You oh God Man seated in heaven/whose life time on earth was humiliated/For our sins, You died on the cross).

24. Titon, *Worlds of Music*, 27.

103 were *nossa música* (NM), forty-two were Portuguese songs (PS), and nine were Western hymns (WH) (see figure 7).

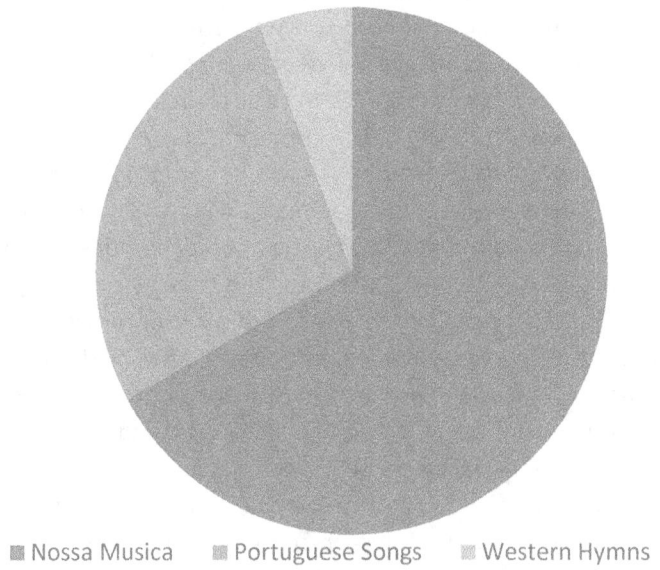

Figure 7: Songs Analyzed

Popular Portuguese songs included, "*Tu és Alfa e Ômega*" (You are Alpha and Omega) and "*Digno És de Gloria*" (You Deserve the Glory), both African American gospel favorites. *Nossa música* (NM) favorites included, "*Mwari Wakanaka*" (God is Good), "*Hakuna Wakaita sa Jesu*" (There is No One Like Jesus), "*Icokwadi Mwari Waripo*" (Surely God is Here), and "*Tinotenda Mware we Masimba*" (Thank You God Most Powerful).

Portuguese songs had a higher text load than *nossa música* songs, of which a majority were antiphonal refrains. Western hymns, with their standard four stanza, four verse form, carried the largest text load of the song styles. In chapter 5, I focus on four key components of the textual analysis, that is the names for God, the metaphors, themes, and song function, and describe how these elements impact believer's affective experience of the music.

Composition and Transmission

Aside from the preservation of missionary legacy through the ongoing use of hymns, songs enter a church's repertory via word of mouth, or in this case, song by mouth. As most worship is led by *jovens* (youth), it is *jovens* who encounter new songs when socializing with friends or visiting other churches, bringing them back to their church to sing. Congregational members too have the right to bring and share songs, sometimes leading out in song at the beginning of service or during offertory.

Composition often occurs in groups, using scripture and salient social issues as the basis for text. Once the text is determined (and generally written down), a melody is found and instruments added to give the song life. At this point composers will record the song, usually on one of the abundant cell phones. Notation or transcription is rarely done as the vast majority of musicians learn aurally. As there is no fixed composition, improvisation is common. Music is organic and communal.

Churches vary on their training methods and musical ability levels. Choirs are a place where members can gain some training as well as a venue for safe socialization with peers in a Christian setting. Particularly in the case of youth choirs, these social organizations are on-ramps for leadership within the church. Most musicians are self-taught, learning by participant observation chiefly through imitation.[25]

Movement

Physical movement (even in the Baptist church) is universal. From kneeling to swaying to clapping to jumping and dancing, movement indicates participation, agreement, and unity. There is a difference in how the *jovens* dance and how the *mães* (moms) or *pastores* (pastors) dance; this likely has to do with age and agility. At the end of the offering at one service, I joined in with the congregation in joyfully dancing around the altar. I tried to keep up with the youthful exuberant jumping and was stiff for the next few days. Though many people commented upon returning to my seat, "You really praised the Lord!"[26] I now dance with the mothers.

---

25. According to the CIA World Fact Book, Mozambique has a literacy rate of 58.8 percent. In addition, it is a highly oral culture, and preferences for oral transmission of data are still evident. Written sheet music is difficult to find, and there is currently only one university that offers a course in music. If one has access to the internet, one can find videos and guitar tabs for music transmission and training.

26. Meyers, field notes, 2013–14.

Gathering the Goats: What Does Worship Look Like in Beira? 67

Figure 8: Processional

Research revealed a marked difference in the performance of the various genres (discussed in greater length in the following chapter). Western hymns were performed at a slow tempo with minimal movement, and there was a noticeable generational variation in participation (older people sang, while younger people were less involved). This was less evident if hymnals were available, as people could read and sing along. Portuguese music tempo varied, but the generational divide in participation was less apparent. Faster songs were accompanied with swaying and clapping, slower songs with closed eyes and raised hands. *Nossa música* was the fastest genre performed. Enthusiastic participation in clapping, ululation, singing, and dancing was manifest among all ages.

Material Aspects of Music

Ninety-two percent of the urban churches visited have some configuration of Western instruments (keyboard, guitar) and a basic sound system (speakers, mic, mixer). Twenty-five percent of the churches also use traditional instruments, *batuques*, tambourines, and other ideophones (rattles, wood blocks, and shakers). When asked about the use of traditional instruments, the response was typically, "We don't have someone that plays them well," or, "It's OK for the rural churches, they don't have the resources we have, but we like these (Western) instruments."[27]

27. Meyers, field notes, 2012–13.

One church rejects traditional instruments completely, citing missionary condemnation, choosing to sing a capella if Western instruments are not available. Ironically, the same informant recognized the inherent duplicity in his church's worship praxis, stating, "Even though we are not allowed to use drums, we are using drums when we use the programmed beats on a keyboard. What's the difference, really?"[28] The preference for Western instruments is a growing trend as more churches have access to electricity and financial resources. This development seems more to be due to *jovens'* (youth's) attraction to pop music and the status of having Western instruments than to a widespread negative stance on traditional instruments and corresponding religious associations.

SUMMARY

In this chapter I have described in detail the current worship praxis in Beira churches, giving generalized demographics, then using Titon's music-performance model from the outside-in to illustrate the music event of worship services. Nascent Mozambican sociocultural values (event orientation and high group values) were evident throughout the worship services. However, foreign mission influence and globalization trends were also demonstrated in the worship song styles and instruments used during services. I now move to a deeper reflection on the impact of Beira's current worship praxis on local believers. Are they grazing and growing through worship?

---

28. Meyers, field notes, 2013–14.

5

Vetting the Herd: Data Analysis

AT THIS STAGE IN the research, I moved to an analysis of the data gathered, answering the question, "What is the impact of current worship praxis on local believers?" I wanted to know if the "goats" were "grazing and growing" in their local church context through worship, or if their discipleship was impeded through the music event of Sunday services.

To answer the above question, I again use Titon's music-performance model (see figure 3) as a framework, now applying it to the impact of current worship praxis on the four arenas, time and space (which includes history), audience and community (social organization), performers and performance (music in use) and finally, music and affective experience (specifically, text).

As in chapter 4, I approach this analysis from the outside-in as it is the history (time and space), social organization (audience and community) and the rules governing how music is performed (performers and performance) that impact the music itself, rather than the other way around. Though music's radiating power is evident, it is the outside influences that determine what, when, how, and why music is played.

TIME AND SPACE: NONCONTEXTUALIZED MISSION HISTORY

Music events such as church services occur not just in a particular setting, time, and space, but are also situated in a historical context. Titon states, "Musical experiences, performances, and communities change over time and space; they have a history, and that history reflects changes in the rules governing music as well as the effect of music on human relationships."[1]

A history of missionary influence, discussed in chapter 1, is clearly evidenced in many aspects of the music event of a worship service in Beira, from the types of songs sung, to the instruments used, the church architecture, dress, and even the performance style of worship leaders.

I turn my attention now to the impact of mission history on worship praxis, unmistakable in the musical repertoire and the use of instruments. Mission history is most evident in Western-initiated churches (WIC), which still sing the Western hymns brought to Mozambique by founding missionaries. Most of these hymns have been translated into either Portuguese or other local languages. Direct translation is problematic in many ways, as King clearly articulates in her dissertation.[2]

First, direct translation can destroy the meaning of the text. Many languages do not fit the meter or melody, leading to profound deviations from the original lyrics or tune, or a distortion of the message. The Portuguese lyrics, for example, to the melody of "O Come All Ye Faithful" are as follows, "*Louvamos, louvamos Senhor e adoramos / A ti oh Deus Homem no çeu asentado / Que em tempo de vida na terra humilhado / Por nossos pecados, morrestes na cruz*" (We praise and worship you, Lord / To You, oh God Man seated in heaven / Who while living on earth was humiliated / For our sins, You died on the cross). Though the end product of this example is still biblical, it was certainly a surprise to me to hear soteriological lyrics set to a Christmas melody.

This distortion can be even more problematic in tonal languages. Though Sena is not a tonal language, Shona, which is related to Ndau, has a high and low tone. Ndau words are always accented on the penultimate syllable, but some songs stress the last syllable, thus having the effect of basically accenting the wrong syllable and distorting the textual meaning. The Ndau hymnbook (*Nduyo joKudira*) includes songs where the translator tried to delete syllables so that the words fit the music. In practice, however, what is written isn't followed. Rather, all the syllables are kept (possibly adding extra notes so that the music fits the words).

Second, hymns may have inappropriate content, including theological concepts that are not currently understood. *Alvo mas que a Neve* (Whiter than Snow), for example, uses imagery that has no contextual

---

1. Titon, *Worlds of Music*, 18.
2. King, *Pathways in Christian Music*, 95–100.

equivalent (*neve*, snow) and poetic vocabulary outside of general use (*alvo*, in common parlance, means goal but can also signify white in poetic prose).

Finally, the foreign music style can be unpleasant, distasteful, or simply just foreign. Though many hymns have been Africanized, or adapted, Western features remain in control.[3] Krabill maintains, "Translated hymns, though perhaps more fully understood than those remaining in a 'foreign' language, are often little more than 'short-cuts,' 'temporary stop-gaps,' and in any case from the point of view of their art, not the best."[4]

For the older generation of believers, hymns, though foreign, remain deeply meaningful as they are the first songs they learned as young believers. However, many *jovens* don't know the hymns, nor care for the musical style. Since most hymnals have nothing more than the words, hymns are threatened by extinction within a generation.

In discussion with me, a pastor bemoaned the fact that his church seems to have no *fogo* (fire) in their worship. I asked him to describe *fogo*. "*Fogo* is the manifest presence of the Holy Spirit, when you can see and feel God's presence in people's faces, in their actions, in their joy, and in their dancing."[5] I then invited him to identify a song his church sings that had *fogo* and one that does not. He selected "*A Mão de Deus é Poderoso*" (The Hand of God is Powerful) and "*Careço de Jesus*" (I Need Thee Every Hour), respectively. Thus, he indicated that a *nossa música* song had *fogo* and a Western hymn did not.

He further explained, "I know that this hymn has good theology, good content, but my congregation doesn't know how to *melgulhar* (dive into) the text."[6] In that moment I realized that, while theologically rich, Western hymns feel foreign and don't connect to Mozambican hearts. Conversely, *nossa música* (NM), though it conveys basic theology, engages people and ignites a passionate response to God. The necessity to reach both the affective and the cognitive dimension through worship music is clear.

Evangelical mission efforts and the rise of Pentecostalism in Mozambique in the early 1990s are manifest in the use of Portuguese songs (PS). This song style, particularly popular with *jovens*, is a foreign style,

3. King, *Music in the Life*, 57–8.
4. Krabill, cited in ibid., 73.
5. Meyers, field notes, 2013–14.
6. Ibid.

though more proximal rhythmically to Mozambican popular music. These songs are imported from Brazil (either translated American, British, or Australian worship songs, or recent compositions by Brazilians). Though the language is the same, the music's country of origin is unmistakable in the music style from the complexity of chord progressions, to rhythmic variations. With increased access and exposure to MTV and YouTube, *jovens* have embraced this song style as their own. However, this style feels particularly foreign to the older generation of Christians.

The fact is, there are very few songs sung in Beira churches that are locally composed. Even *nossa música* (NM) is largely imported music from neighboring Malawi, Zimbabwe, or South Africa and then sometimes translated into local languages. NM feels closer to home musically (for both generations of believers), but likely has not originated in the city.

Regional variations in *nossa música* (NM) confound the issue of contextualization. Though the music may have originated in another locale, it has been locally appropriated and recontextualized. A national survey to discover regional music preferences is beyond the scope of this study. Yet it is clear that people have made NM their own.

This is actually a point of debate among Mozambicans themselves, as Mozambique has always been a cross-road of cultures, nowhere more evident than in music. There are those that take the position that Mozambican music is only that which uses styles and rhythms that are accepted as being Mozambican. Others hold the view that culturally acceptable Mozambican music is that which is composed by a Mozambican, irrespective of the style and rhythm of origin.

Particularly in the context of a worship service, I contend that the priority remains the performance of music that speaks from the heart of local believers in a local church community to the heart of God. It is what Cherry defines as "convergence worship," that is, "the combining of the historical and the contemporary at every level of worship to create maximum opportunities for engaging worshippers with the presence of God."[7]

My main concern is not whether or not music is foreign or Mozambican, but whether or not the local body of believers can connect with God's presence in worship through a particular song style. Unfortunately, the use of either Western hymns or Portuguese songs excludes a slice of the congregation. *Nossa música* (NM), on the other hand, while

---

7. Cherry, *Worship Architect*, 248.

it can also be argued as foreign, has become Mozambican, embraced by all. "Let's sing *nossa música*; it really gets the congregation going!"[8] NM's ubiquitous presence across denominational lines attests to its ability to engage the entire congregation.

Traditional Mozambican instruments are rarely used, due either to missionary condemnation, or to appropriation and imitation of contemporary worship bands. One church clearly articulated historical missional influence on the rejection of traditional instruments. When I asked a worship leader and research partner why Beira churches use Western instruments, he replied, "It is complicated. Early missionaries duplicated their home churches and made Xerox copies here. They told us our culture is sinful, that we can't use our language and our instruments to call God."[9]

This stands to reason, one calls a new god with different instruments. Yet the devastating legacy of devaluing and discrediting Mozambican musical heritage, inculcated by missionaries, continues in the attitudes and behaviors of Mozambican youth. "I adore Jesus Culture, their music really helps me worship," reported one *joven*.[10] As songs are imported (or imposed in new church plants), so are the instruments to replicate not only the lyrics but also the musical style.

History still plays a significant role in what music is played and what instruments are used in Beira churches today. The largely noncontextualized mission strategy, particularly in relation to music, further exacerbated by globalization, has saddled Mozambican believers with a foreign worship style making it difficult to fully engage in a transformational worship experience. Churches are splintered into generational factions articulated along musical preferences, impeding unity and communal growth. Discipleship through worship is hindered by a legacy of noncontextualized worship arts praxis.

AUDIENCE AND COMMUNITY: SOCIAL HIERARCHY

Another influential factor on worship music is the worshipping community, defined by Titon as "the group (including performers) that carries on the traditions and norms of performance."[11] In Beira, worship leading

---

8. Meyers, field notes, 2012–13.
9. Meyers, field notes, 2013–14.
10. Ibid.
11. Titon, *Worlds of Music*, 18.

is almost exclusively within the purview of *jovens*. "Music is something the youth do before the pastor gets up to preach."[12] Sometimes this occurs via a designated worship group, but more often through a youth choir. While there are a few exceptions, a young worship leader or youth choir is considered normative in worship through music.

Yet, Mozambican culture sees *jovens* as people who have not yet reached full maturity. They are still young and gaining wisdom that comes from life experiences. This is concurrent with the surrounding authoritarian society in which age confers status and respect. *Jovens* are placed in positions of musical leadership with neither training nor cultural capital in order to lead with authority.

Following the worship through music portion of the service, I've heard *dirigintes do culto* (MCs) announce the preaching portion of the service by saying, "This (the sermon) is the most important part of the service."[13] The MC is essentially discrediting the entire first half of the service. A few young worship leaders expressed feelings of frustration with this practice, saying, "I feel like everything we just did is in vain, that the church doesn't appreciate our efforts."[14] This practice devalues not only *jovens* but also the worship experience through music itself.

Other conversations with worship leaders revealed a reticence to approach the pastors to ask for sermon topics due to generational respect and a non-crisis cultural orientation (low uncertainty avoidance). "What's the point of planning when the preacher changes his topic or a visitor is asked to preach instead? Let's not let people know what the topics are so that they won't be disappointed."[15]

Titon states, "How the community relates to the music makers also has a profound effect on the music."[16] Communication theory reiterates this idea, postulating that the medium of communication is inextricably intertwined with the message itself. Smith argues, "The communicator is the container, and the container inevitably shapes the message."[17]

Since the leadership of *jovens* (the medium) is undermined by societal conventions, it also weakens the potential impact of the music

---

12. Meyers, field notes, 2012–13.
13. Meyers, field notes, 2013–14.
14. Meyers, field notes, 2014–15.
15. Meyers, field notes, 2013–14.
16. Titon, *Worlds of Music*, 18.
17. Smith, *Creating Understanding*, 105.

(message) on the congregation, as the older congregants are hesitant to receive instruction from youth. "What you are speaks so loudly, I cannot hear what you are saying."[18] It is clear that Mozambican social hierarchy greatly impacts the leadership effectiveness of young musicians, and weakens the transformational effect of worship music on the church community as a whole.

PERFORMERS AND PERFORMANCE: FRACTURED WORSHIP

Performers, in this case, primarily *jovens*, bring music into being through performance. Performance, as defined by Titon, incorporates many things. "First, people mark performances as separate from the flow of ordinary life.... Second, performance has purpose.... Third, performance is interpreted as it goes along."[19] While calling the music event of a worship service a performance may be distasteful to some within the evangelical tradition, I simply use this term as a means of conveying how the music is embodied in the church service, how it "moves along on the basis of agreed-upon rules and procedures."[20]

The music event performance at a Beira church inevitably starts with someone in the congregation starting to sing. How they know when to start is still beyond me, a time-oriented person, as services rarely start at the indicated time. Sometimes someone rings a bell. Other churches begin a service by loudly and collectively praying. Regardless of the means, music (or some type of meaningfully organized sound) marks the beginning of a church service. It is a signal to all that the service has started.

Music not only begins the event, but it mediates virtually every portion of the service, from special musical presentations by choirs, to offering, to announcements and testimonies. Music even fills in the cracks, the dead space of transitions, when someone is coming to the front, or when there is a technical problem, or when people are leaving to prepare for a processional. It keeps the service flowing, and provides a sense of continuity through change.

Every pastor I spoke with agreed that worship (implying music) was a vital part of church life. Pastor Lázaro simply stated, "Worship is

18. Ibid., 104.
19. Titon, *Worlds of Music*, 17.
20. Ibid.

important. When we worship, God is in our midst."[21] The primary purpose of the worship performance, then, is to enter into God's presence, "*Vamos entrar na presença de Deus!*" (Let's go into God's presence). A corollary purpose is to invoke God's manifest presence, particularly prior to preaching, "We'll sing one more strong and alive song to call God's presence before the sermon."[22]

There is a general belief that there is a marked difference between the singing and the sermon. The performance is interpreted two ways. Worship is either considered to be only the music, "Now we're done with worship,"[23] or the sermon is elevated, "Now we've come to the most important part of the service."[24] There is no sense of cohesion, little to no connection or consistency between the music and the spoken message.

Sermon themes ranged from missions, to obedience, to spiritual battle, to the resurrection and the reign of God. Yet the song selection rarely if ever reflected the sermon themes. When I asked my research assistants about it they said:

> This is a big issue, it's a matter of lack of planning and poor communication between the pastor and the worship team. We (worship teams) rarely know what the sermon will be about, and there's often last minute changes, suddenly an evangelist comes to town and is asked to preach, or someone doesn't show up to play an instrument which means we have to eliminate a song, or the power's out, or a guitar's strings are broken.[25]

The idea of a comprehensive worship service that includes singing, offering, preaching, that all parts of the service are a form of worship, is a foreign concept. Based on my research, I would describe a Mozambican philosophy of worship music performance as an alarm clock, a space filler, and an emotional outlet. One research partner bluntly said:

> People come to church to get something from God, rather than to meet with Him and render him the praise that He is due. If you were to paint a sign, "Come, bring your sacrifice of praise" above the door of a church, no one would come. But if you were

---

21. Meyers, field notes, 2012–13.
22. Ibid.
23. Meyers, field notes, 2013–14.
24. Ibid.
25. Ibid.

to paint, "Come receive your miracle here," you'd have a church full of people.[26]

This prevailing philosophy is due to traditional religious beliefs about the motivation for spiritual interaction and to the "low church" Pentecostal missiology, which inclines toward the sentiment, "Let the spirit lead," meaning little to no forethought or liturgical planning. An allergy to all things Catholic further contributes to an avoidance of rigid ritual performance. While there are times when the presence of the Lord is clearly felt, there are many other moments where worship (specifically music) is far less than a dialogue with the Divine.

Rather than cohesively reiterating spiritual truths and concepts through the intentional use of multiple communication channels, thereby increasing understanding and the possibility of growth, current worship performance in evangelical churches in Beira is determined by personal preference and ability: "everyone did as they saw fit" (Judg 17:6b). Unfortunately, this philosophy hinders discipleship, as it leads to a consumeristic interpretation of worship, "What's in it for me?" rather than a submissive surrender to the transformational presence of God, evidenced in a life of obedience and service.

MUSIC AND AFFECTIVE EXPERIENCE: FORM AND FUNCTION INHIBIT LEARNING

Having demonstrated how each aspect of music-culture impacts the music itself, I now hone in on music's affect, its radiating power to move people. Here, I specifically focus in on the song texts and emotional impact these song texts have on the people who sing them. As stated in chapter 4, I conducted summative content analysis on 154 songs from nine different churches. Of the total number of songs, 103 were *nossa música* (NM), 42 were Portuguese songs (PS), and 9 were Western hymns (WH) (see figure 7, chapter 4). I (along with my two research assistants) filled in the analysis Table 3 for each song set.

---

26. Ibid.

Table 3: Sample Content Analysis Form

Title	Trinity	Scriptures	Metaphors	Themes	God?	Us?	Function
Torai Vhangeri		Matt 28:19–20	Gospel				exhort
Munamato Una Simba	God=3	Jonah, Daniel	Waters, dry things	Prayer		Pray through difficulties	exhort
Mwari Ndinoda	Lord=2 Jesus=1	Oil – 10 virgins? Fire in bones – Jer 20:9	Oil in heart	Passion	Jesus is returning	Be ready	prayer

Allow me to focus on four key components of the analysis: names for God, metaphors, themes, and song function. Out of the 154 songs analyzed, the Trinity was mentioned twice, and the Holy Spirit 13 times, though all of the churches have a trinitarian doctrine, and 75 percent have Pentecostal inclinations (Table 4). What this indicated was an inconsistency between the stated denominational proclivity and the preached word, and what was being affirmed each week in song. Though churches said they are Pentecostal, they rarely sang about the work of the Holy Spirit in their lives.

As metaphors "are central to the functioning of culture texts, especially those . . . that express in a special way the structures of identities,"[27] I wanted to gain an understanding of what identities were being formed through the use of metaphors in song. Metaphors were variable, though many came from the Old Testament (Lion of tribe of Judah, Hope of Israel). Of the songs analyzed, *evangelho* (Good News—specifically the gospel) was mentioned eleven times. Royal metaphors (crown, king, throne room) were also popular, particularly in Portuguese songs. Natural metaphors (rock, water, storm, sea, watering dry land) also occurred repeatedly. These metaphors seem consistent with the Mozambican sense of connection to the land and to a hierarchal social structure.

27. Schreiter, *Constructing Local Theologies*, 69.

Table 4: Names for God

Names for God	Frequency
Jesus	96
Lord	95
God	68
Father	33
Holy Spirit	13
Christ/Savior	23
Trinity	2
Jehovah	2

Themes, like metaphors, had significant variation, necessitating a further grouping into larger subject categories or "meta-themes." As illustrated in Table 5, most subjects had multiple themes. For example, themes for the subject of offering included, "God deserves our offering," and "We should bring offerings." The subject of believers had the greatest number of theological themes, but the subject of God Father was most frequently referenced.[28]

Table 5: Song Subjects, Themes, and Frequency

Subject	Themes	Frequency
God (Father)	21	92
Jesus	18	60
Holy Spirit	6	7
Believers	27	56
Church	1	1
After-life	3	4
Baptism	2	2
Evangelism	4	11
Offering	2	3
Prayer	4	6
TOTAL	88	242

28. For a complete record of the subjects, themes, and frequency broken down by song types, please see Appendix F.

In figure 9, I demonstrate the number of themes covered in each song style, showing that *nossa música* (NM) covers the most theological principles of the three song styles. However, when one compares the theological themes to the number of songs in each style, one quickly realizes that the ratios show a very different picture.

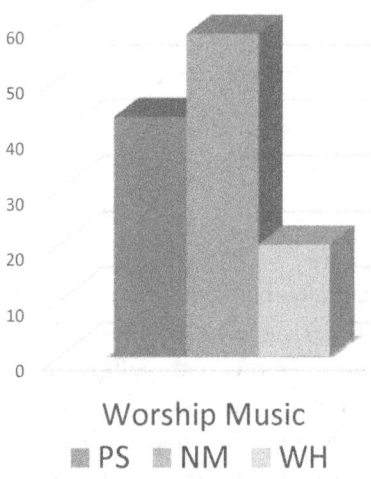

Portuguese Songs (PS), 42 songs, 43 themes (~1:1 ratio) = 102%
Nossa Música (NM), 103 songs, 58 themes (~2:1 ratio) = 56%
Western Hymns (WH), 9 songs, 20 themes (~1:2 ratio) = 222%

Figure 9: Themes per Song Style

In other words, Western hymns carry four times more text load and theological themes as a song style (genre) than *nossa música*. Research shows that the time spent singing each type of song and the number of songs sung at each service is roughly equivalent, regardless of the genre. This means that churches that sing primarily *nossa música* are being exposed to one-quarter of the theological concepts sung by churches that prefer Western hymns. The couplet refrain form of Beira churches' preferred genre, *nossa música*, impedes discipleship through lyric theology.

A final area of consideration for the song collections was to explore each song's primary function. Authors have differing lists for the functions of music, with some convergence, from Donald Hustad (1981) to Corbitt (1998). Initial pilot testing revealed liturgical function codes that most closely matched Cherry's list: "proclamation, prayer, praise, exhortation, and call to action."[29] As a research team, we agreed to choose from the following list of options: gather, praise, prayer, proclamation, exhort, and send-out. We also delineated the functions per song styles, *nossa música* (NM), Western hymns (WH), and Portuguese songs (PS).

Table 6: Song Functions

Function:	NM	WH	PS	total
Gathering	2	0	0	2
Praise	22	2	15	38
Prayer	7	2	8	17
Proclamation	45	3	1	66
Exhortation	27	3	1	31
Send-Out	0	0	0	0
Total:	103	9	42	154

From the results in Table 6, it is clear that certain song styles favor particular functions. *Nossa música* favored proclamation, while Portuguese songs leaned toward praise. Noting that *nossa música* style comprised roughly two-thirds of the worship songs analyzed, it is not surprising then that 43 percent of the song functions were proclamation, followed by praise at 25 percent, exhortation at 20 percent, and finally prayer at 11 percent. The gathering function was only used twice and none of the songs analyzed commissioned or sent-out worshippers.

A simple word-based technique of counting repeated words shows areas of primacy or importance in the minds of those who speak (or in this case, sing) them. D'Andre notes that "perhaps the simplest and most direct indication of schematic organization in naturalistic discourse is the repetition of associative linkages."[30] Therefore, by looking both at what is frequently repeated and also at what is not present in the song texts analyzed, one can discover underlying cultural values.

For example, missionary sources inform me that there is no word for Trinity in Ndau or in Sena. This was evident in the songs analyzed, as only one song (a Portuguese song) mentioned the Trinity twice. Therefore,

---

29. Cherry, *Worship Architect*, 189.
30. D'Andre, *Development of Cognitive Anthropology*, 294.

although all cases researched believed in a Triune God, there was a profound weakness in trinitarian lyric theology.[31] On the other hand, praise is an important traditional means of showing honor and respect to elders, leaders, ancestors, and gods. It is therefore not surprising that this value is also mirrored repeatedly in evangelical worship music.

The preferred form (short refrain of *nossa música*) and preferred function (proclivity toward proclamation and praise) of the most frequently sung songs in the churches studied demonstrate that Mozambican believers enjoy God's presence, power, and praising Him, but know little of how to live their lives beyond Sunday, how to walk in victory and faithful discipleship from Monday through Saturday.

SUMMARY

I have yet to meet a Mozambican who does not enjoy music and dancing. That being said, while everyone is supportive and appreciative of worship arts, I believe it is still quite underutilized in ministry and mission. Music mediates church services and is ubiquitous both in and out of the church. However, it is not intentionally used as a tool for transformation.

In this chapter, I have demonstrated that a noncontextualized mission history and globalization in Mozambique has led to the burden of a foreign worship style. I have shown how the authoritarian social hierarchy has undermined young worship leaders and the reception of the musical message in the hearts of the older congregants. I have discussed a Mozambican philosophy of music and performance that inhibits learning, and I have argued that the form and function of the most popular music style in Beira churches is limiting exposure to theological concepts. The lack of teaching and practice of contextualized worship arts in the development of disciples in Beira churches is clear.

This communication and training deficiency extends beyond worship planning or the types of songs sung. In fact, the Mozambican church in general does not see discipleship as a priority. Instead, the emphasis appears to be on giving (generosity), singing, and community (respect

---

31. For those who can read and have access to the Sena catechism, they can find an adequate description of the Trinity as follows: *Alipo Mulungu m'bodzi basi, Mulungu wa m'maso na wa undimomwene, mbapangizika m'mawonekero matatu—Baba, Mwana, na Nzimu wakucena. Mu utatu wawo ndi Mulungu m'bodzi, mwa makhaliro mabodziene, mwa mphambvu na mbiri ibodziene* (There is one God only, a God who is alive and is true, and is shown in three appearances—Father, Son and Holy Spirit. In the three there is one God with one character and same strength and glory).

for elders and husbands, being loving and supportive to each other, and avoiding gossip). These values are reflected in the culture at large, and reinforced by the songs sung, the topics preached, and in other learning opportunities (Bible studies, Sunday school, and small groups), though these venues seem to have varying levels of success.

Some pastors bemoaned the fact that there didn't seem to be much interest in discipleship, claiming that the "distractions of technology and preoccupation with survival" were a greater priority to their flock than learning about God's Word.[32] Yet their authoritarian leadership style itself sometimes limited *jovens* from participating in worship training opportunities for fear of attrition or "sheep stealing." Pastors are the power brokers in Beira churches and, as I soon discovered, were the key to worship transformation in the local body of believers.

As I entered the third phase of my research, initiating adaptive change, I knew I needed to address these issues. How could I encourage the development of songs whose form and function allowed for greater exposure to a complete gospel? What would encourage pastors and worship leaders to work together to form a cohesive service that engendered greater learning? How could I break decades of cultural demoralization and inspire Mozambican praise? I focus next on these questions in part three, explaining my methodology and subsequent findings and results assessments.

---

32. Meyers, field notes, 2013–14.

Part Three

Grazing and Growing: Adaptive Change through Worship Praxis

In Part Two, I examined my research data, demonstrating a lack of teaching and practice of contextualized worship arts in Beira churches. A noncontextualized mission history, social hierarchy, fractured worship, and the form and function of the most popular worship song style inhibited the development of local disciples. The need for a functional model of indigenous hymnody was abundantly clear.

In Part Three, I describe how I addressed the above issues and assessed the outcomes in the third and fourth phases of my research. Chapter 6, "Songwriting Workshop Method Expanded and Applied," details the expanded songwriting workshop model and its application in Beira, while chapter 7, "Results Assessment: What Happened?" evaluates the impact of these adaptive change methods on the development of church ministry and mission in Beira churches.

6

Songwriting Workshop Method Expanded and Applied

> Silence ... punctuated by hushed conversations, tentative thoughts shared between group members, characterizes the start of a composing session. Heads huddled together around Bibles and notebooks, the participants lean in to each other as they listen to the scriptures and begin talking about the theological themes, deciding on salient sentences that form the basis for song.
>
> As I wander from group to group, I start to hear sounds, a hummed refrain, a suggested couplet, a burst of laughter as two participants inadvertently blurt out a melody at once. It is like making musical popcorn ... crescendo-ing from silence to a cacophony of sound as more and more ideas surface and are shaped by group members, some run to grab a guitar or begin to add clapping and harmony as a song develops.
>
> Soon it becomes so loud that some groups move away from the others so that they can hold on to their melody even as other songs are simultaneously produced. Smiles are everywhere. It is time to harvest the musical fruit.[1]

---

1. Meyers, composer's club description, field notes, 2013–14.

Songwriting workshops are a methodological practice of ethnodoxology, successfully conducted in numerous settings around the globe.[2] One of the strengths of this particular method (allowing participants to lead in the creation of indigenous hymnody) is, in some cases, its weakness. This method assumes that local composers are qualified musicians and theologians, creating songs that are biblically solid and culturally relevant, and that they have the relationships and authority to encourage the use of new songs in local church worship. Sometimes this is the case, and incredible church growth is the result. However, there are times when many new songs are started that aren't brought to maturity, never getting sung to bring about transformation.

My concern throughout this research was to make disciples, through contextualized worship arts, that in turn developed church ministry and mission. Therefore, the effectiveness of my primary change method, songwriting workshops, was paramount. I needed to discover how to reframe the method to fit the research context, and to modify the method in order to maximize sustainable adaptive change through worship praxis.

I quickly discovered that affecting transformation was far more complex than just getting people to beat on a *batuque* and sing in their mother tongue, for in a majority of my urban church contexts traditional instruments weren't used. Some younger congregants preferred Portuguese songs, a foreign music style, while older congregants in mainline churches were deeply engaged in singing Western hymns.

I had to wrestle with questions of personal motivation. Was I more interested in preserving and promoting a music-culture that, in many ways, was excluded from current worship practice or in fostering engaged worshippers, who were transformed through worship, even if it meant singing foreign songs? If Mozambicans had appropriated foreign music as a means of dialogue with the Divine, who was I (a foreigner) to impose Mozambican music-culture onto current worship practice? In insisting on home music, was I not in some ways just repeating the mistake of earlier missionaries, imposing a worship style on Mozambican Christians?

Participant observation at my twelve cases revealed songs-in-use. I recorded not only the types of songs being sung from week to week at various churches, but how they were being sung. I observed levels of congregational participation and experienced the flow of worship and the

---

2. See King, *Music in the Life*; Higashi, "Musical Communitas"; Scott, *Moving Into African Music*; and Schrag and Krabill, *Creating Local Arts Together*.

presence of the Holy Spirit throughout the liturgy. I learned that worship as currently defined in practice is the songs sung during service.

Interviews with pastors, worship leaders, and congregants revealed the generational challenges between youth and church leadership. Youth expressed frustration at being given the ministry task of leading worship, but not the authority to carry out the task. Pastors shared concern about the lifestyle of youth and their desire to move too far too fast. I learned of numerous accounts of moral failure and noted a paucity of training opportunities.

Finally, content analysis of frequently sung songs uncovered the challenge of a popular song form (*nossa música*) that, while musically at home, was limited by its form (low text load) and function (proclamation and praise). People needed songs that engaged not just their hearts but also their heads. Content analysis also revealed holes in local theology, only a limited amount of songs touched on the life of Christ, and what it means to be a disciple. Congregants were not singing the whole gospel.

It was abundantly clear that I would have to do more than one songwriting workshop in each church context if I was going to hope to achieve adaptive change through worship praxis. It would require building relationships with pastors, attempting to bridge the divide between youth and church leadership by engaging the power brokers in the change process. Numerous training opportunities for worship leaders and musicians were also necessary, not just teaching new methods but mentoring them, providing worship labs for experimenting and trying new ways to worship. I needed to develop a multipronged expanded approach, tailored to each church's felt needs and desires.

TIME AND SPACE: SONGWRITING WORKSHOP METHOD EXPANDED AND APPLIED IN BEIRA

In this chapter, then, applying Titon's music-performance model as a frame, I explain how I expanded and applied the songwriting workshop methodology as a means of encouraging the use of contextualized worship arts in Beira churches from January to August of 2014. This contextualized experimental methodology, based on my prior context research, was designed to initiate adaptive change. I therefore drew heavily upon the works of Heifitz and Linsky (*Leadership On the Line*) and Parks (*Leadership Can Be Taught*), which describe the practice of adaptive leadership, and the works of Lingenfelter (*Leading Cross-Culturally*), and Plueddemann (*Leading Across Cultures*), which focus on leading cross-culturally.

Adaptive Change Methodology

I was committed to mentoring people through the change, rather than managing the change myself, and so I had to develop strategies that would allow for collaborative leadership, aiding pastors and worship leaders to "get on the balcony" to see what was really happening in their church contexts, and to "think politically." I was obliged, therefore, to "orchestrate the conflict" in each aspect of the music-culture of Beira churches.[3] This included initiating focus group interviews and creating holding environments, or safe spaces, where participants could creatively consider changing current worship praxis through genuine dialogue and "case-in-point" learning.

As the leader of these training opportunities in holding environments I had to "control the temperature" of the discussions to foster genuine dialogue, bringing *batata quente* (hot potato) questions to the group, encouraging each person to participate. I also had to "pace the work" by refereeing the discussions, challenging participants to consider new ideas and backing off when the group seemed overwhelmed. Finally, I "showed the future" in the form of videos from other contexts to inspire vision beyond present reality. These aspects of the training opportunities enabled participants to embody comprehensive contextual change.

Experimental Interventions

I was concerned not only with initiating adaptive change through an expanded songwriting workshop model in collaboration with participating churches, but also in assessing the results of the variables presented to churches. In other words, I wanted to understand if there was a causal relationship between contextualized worship arts (independent variable) and church ministry and mission (dependent variable). Therefore, I needed to find an experimental design method that would track the effect of an intervention on multiple groups over a period of time. This most closely correlated with a multiple baseline design.[4]

---

3. Heifetz and Linsky, *Leadership on the Line*, 771, 1135, 1544–889.
4. Leedy and Ellis Ormrod, *Practical Research*, 244.

The independent variable consisted of numerous factors, a focus group interview (presented at a different time to each church), and training opportunities in holding environments (three worship leaders' small group meetings, three composer's clubs, twelve jam sessions, and twelve vocal training class sessions). All these factors were presented over the course of three months, from February to April 2014; though the composer's clubs, jam sessions, and worship leaders' small group continued in my absence from the research context from April to August 2014. As participation in the training opportunities was voluntary, there were many churches that did not participate fully in this third phase of research, one case (Nova Alliança) inadvertently becoming a control because it was not exposed to any experimental interventions.

My site visits to each church during Phase II provided me with baseline data about each group. I then conducted focus group interviews (one factor of the independent variable) at a different time for each group (see Table 7). Scheduling the focus group interviews was a random selection process after pilot-testing the method at Família Vitoriosa (VFC), my primary case site. I called all the pastors of participating churches in January and began scheduling interview dates, with twelve weekends and twelve focus groups to organize, this was no small feat. I was unfortunately unable to schedule focus group interviews with three churches (NA, ADA, and ADI) in the allotted three-month time frame.

Table 7: Focus Group Interviews Timetable

Church	Feb			March				April	
VFC	X	O	O	O	O	O	O	O	O
VPD	O	X	O	O	O	O	O	O	O
MEVN	O	O	X	O	O	O	O	O	O
AM	O	O	O	X	O	O	O	O	O
AB	O	O	O	O	X	O	O	O	O
1stB	O	O	O	O	O	X	O	O	O
ADE	O	O	O	O	O	O	X	O	O
UB	O	O	O	O	O	O	O	X	O
ECD	O	O	O	O	O	O	O	O	X

Key: O: Observations; X: Focus Group Interview

The research corpus for Phase III included:

1. Participant observation: 13 church services, 11 site visits, 3 music events, 11 rehearsals/meetings, 3 composer's clubs, 12 jam sessions, 3 worship leaders' small group, 12 voice technique classes
2. Interviews (focus groups): 9 churches
3. Experimental interventions in holding environments: 12 voice technique classes, 12 jam sessions, 3 worship leaders' small group, 3 composer's clubs.

In the following sections, I discuss the methods used in Phase III, created to address each of Titon's domains. I start with focus group interviews that engaged the church community through critically reflexive discussions. I then move to describe training opportunities in holding environments; experimental interventions geared specifically toward worship leaders and their performance during church services. Finally, I depict the monthly composer's clubs (another type of holding environment) in which we developed new music.

AUDIENCE AND COMMUNITY: FOCUS GROUP INTERVIEWS

As mentioned above, the multipronged applied experimental research phase was initiated with a focus group interview of church leaders (pastors, elders, and worship leaders) in each participating church context, where I facilitated a reflexive discussion of their current worship praxis. As context research revealed a fault-line between pastors and younger worship leaders, I chose to initiate the change experiments with focus group.

My goal in using this method was to build on effective group think that allowed them to share and bond together with a purpose, and, in so doing, begin to bridge the divide between generational factions. Focus groups of mixed ages recognized the authoritarian and highly communal cultural context. By respecting older leadership, rather than ignoring or subverting it, the focus groups helped get older leaders on board with the change process. These discussions engaged them as change agents, thus increasing the likelihood of lasting sustainable change in each church context.

During these meetings I first led a small meditation based on Matt 5:14–16 and explained that we'd be watching a video of their church service (created from site visits in Phase II). I asked them to watch the video with the following question in mind, "Is this worship practice shining the light of Christ to the world or is it hiding or putting out His light?"

The video compilation of one of the services served as a concrete discussion aid, giving participants a chance to auto-critique and to clarify and confirm what I had witnessed in Phase II. This technique was congruent with adaptive change methodology and a participatory action research (PAR) stance, in which "participants (are) engaged in collaborative processes aimed at improving and understanding their worlds in order to change them."[5] My questioning route after watching the video was as follows:

a. What did you see in the video (or know to be true about your church) that shines the light of Christ? What worship practices are positive? How can we continue this positive practice?

b. What did you see in the video (or know to be true about your church) that hides or puts out the light of Christ? What worship practices are negative (need to be improved)? How can we improve or avoid these negative practices?

c. What practical steps will we take from here to meet these challenges?

Participants deliberated about the pros and cons of their current worship practice, and articulated the challenges they were facing.

Pastors, together with worship leaders and elders then determined an action plan for change in worship, coming up with at least two goals for the year. These concrete next steps helped to focus efforts and to gauge the transformative progress. Many churches opted to utilize the various training opportunities I offered, composer's clubs, worship classes, jam sessions, and a worship leaders' small group. The focus groups served to not only build trust, but also to galvanize the church leadership to action.

PERFORMERS AND PERFORMANCE: TRAINING OPPORTUNITIES IN HOLDING ENVIRONMENTS

As training was a major need, expressed by all pastors of participating churches in the structured interviews (Phase II), I employed multiple "holding environments" to orchestrate adaptive change through training.[6]

5. McIntyre, *Participatory Action Research*, 36.

6. Heifetz and Linsky encourage leaders to create safe spaces where participants can launch strategic initiatives through genuine dialogue with each other. "Remember your job is to orchestrate the conflict, not become it. You need to let people do the

These experimental training opportunities, off-site from participating church contexts,[7] allowed for social cohesion and cross-fertilization of ideas across denominational lines, and engendered freedom to experiment and gain capacity in new practices.

The holding environments included a twelve-week voice technique course, weekly jam sessions, monthly composer's clubs at Família Vitoriosa (VFC), and monthly worship leaders' meetings at Instituto Bíblico de Sofala (IBS). Though each experimental environment had a different focus, and engaged different groups of people, each session focused on facilitating adaptive change, empowering participants as a group to lead the change in their own church context. Below I describe the holding environments (jam sessions, worship leaders' small group, and seminary classes and chapels) before moving on to composer's clubs. Each of these interventions, to varying degrees, have continued since their inception in early 2014.

Jam Sessions

Twelve weekly jam sessions, initially conceived as a means for performance ethnography with local musicians, quickly evolved into a small group of Christian musicians from various churches with a two-fold purpose, to expand their musical capacity of *nossa música* and other local music-forms, and to share their faith in song. After two months of building a relatively consistent core of participants and a repertoire, we started performing publicly.

Our first public foray was at the entrance to the Central Hospital of Beira, a highly trafficked area that includes a *chapa* (bus) stop and an ATM. Our presence drew the attention of a local radio station that did a live interview with a colleague. The interviewer, a blind Muslim, was befuddled at the fact that multiple churches could come together to publicly proclaim peace found in Jesus.

Other venues for this ongoing music ministry included Casa de Cultura, a local cultural arts performance center, and various *chapa* stops

---

work that only they can do" (Heifetz and Linsky, *Leadership On the Line*, 1889).

7. The one exception to this off-site practice was the composer's clubs at Família Vitoriosa (my primary case). However, as Pastor João actively participated in these clubs and diligently worked at affecting adaptive change through the worship ministry, this didn't appear to be hindering freedom to change. Conversely, holding the composer's clubs on-site lent a seriousness and credibility to Pastor João's change efforts, and encouraged greater membership participation.

around the city. The group not only sings, but also preaches and prays with people passing by. Observers are reported to be converting and, when possible, are linked to pastors and local churches for follow-up discipleship. The group leader, Djongue, is a passionate Christian musician who feels called to minister to fellow musicians who might never darken the door of a church. Group participants grew in confidence, and their perspective about evangelism and missions has expanded.

Worship Leaders' Small-Group

The need for discipleship and leadership training of worship leaders became blatantly obvious through my context research (Phase II). Both pastors and worship leaders expressed a desire for mentoring and for community. Having received permission to use a room from Instituto Bíblico de Sofala (IBS), an interdenominational seminary and therefore neutral territory, a small group of worship leaders from multiple churches met once a month for three months to pray, worship, and learn together. For many it was a powerful antidote to feelings of isolation and hopelessness.

At our second meeting I asked a Mozambican musician and missionary, Manuel Mário, to lead a devotional based off of Isa 6:1–4. The discussion of the arc of worship as outlined in the passage was rich and convicting for participants. We then explored other Bible passages about worship, and discovered that there is biblical precedence for critical contextualization in worship. One participant exclaimed, "You mean, we can actually use our traditional instruments to worship God?"[8]

By the third meeting the mantle of leadership was placed on Manuel Mário's shoulders. He defined critical contextualization based on Matt 24:14 and Rom 1:14–16, and engaged the group in a Socratic discussion about the blessings and challenges of the missionary legacy in Mozambique. Participants explored together the freedoms and responsibilities the local church now has to define appropriate and meaningful worship. The ensuing dialogue was animated and no one wanted to leave when the time was done. Everyone expressed the importance of ongoing group meetings for them personally and for the Mozambican church at large. These leaders continue to meet for mutual encouragement and accountability.

---

8. Meyers, field notes, 2013–14.

Vocal Technique Class

One consistent area of need highlighted in the focus group interview was musical training. I therefore taught a twelve-week vocal technique course at the Baptist Seminary to a class of about twenty students, over half were audit students who'd been invited to join as part of the action points developed in focus groups. Each class was taught using "case-in-point" methodology with a loose working curriculum. Though I had concepts I wanted to teach each week, I built the class work as we went along, basing my teaching points on students' attendance and skill level.

The final concert was a "sung service" during the seminary's regularly scheduled chapel hour. Our repertoire included a Western hymn, Portuguese songs, *nossa música*, and even an arranged version of Handel's "Hallelujah Chorus." Manuel Mário, my teaching assistant and accompanist, also preached a sermon about music and missions based on Isa 6:1–8. Students invited their families, friends, and pastors to attend. It was a packed house. The hosting pastor enjoyed the service so much he invited the group to perform the same concert during his Sunday service two weeks later.

Having described how I expanded my experimental change methodology to include focus groups and other training opportunities, I now move to explain the application of the songwriting workshop method in Beira, Mozambique, monthly composer's clubs. These clubs, like the jam sessions, voice classes, and small groups, were also training opportunities in a holding environment. However, as composer's clubs are a major method of ethnodoxology, and as my primary research goal was to discover ways to expand the model, I pay particular attention to my rationale for the methodological variations I applied in this study below.

MUSIC AND AFFECTIVE EXPERIENCE: COMPOSER'S CLUBS

> We're not just having another meeting where we talk and do nothing, these workshops have tangible results![9]

Ethnodoxology is still far from being fully used in missiology, particularly in Africa. While some incredible strides have been taken, there is still much work to be done, both in terms of actually engaging

---

9. Meyers, workshop participant, field notes, 2013–14.

ethnodoxology as a full-fledged partner in ministry efforts, but also in terms of grounding methodology in sound academic research that critically seeks to improve and build on existing praxis. This research sought to explore and expand the capacity of the songwriting workshop, a central ethnodoxology method.

King, Higashi, and Scott have effectively used this methodology to create indigenous hymnody.[10] However, in the interest of efficiency and time, and due to a genuine desire to allow cultural "experts" to lead the creation of indigenous hymnody, some ethnodoxologists have fired a "shot in the dark" with the songwriting workshop model (myself included). They enter a cultural context "blind" and trust that the songs created will be used to bless and edify the church. While this method quickly produces new scripture songs, I am more concerned with the long-term use of the new songs in the church and the effects on sustainable church growth, ministry, and missions. Are churches really singing their new songs and are people's lives being transformed as a result?

The cross-case research design of this study gave me an understanding of the "thick description" of the context in which the songwriting workshops occurred and allowed me to build strong relationships with pastors and worship leaders. This circumvented the "shot in the dark" songwriting workshop approach, revealing numerous factors that compelled me to alter the change process strategy into a multipronged approach, tailor-made for each church context in partnership with church leadership (described above). I also discovered that I needed to modify the workshop method itself, increasing the frequency of workshops, enriching the events with teaching components, and expanding the potential influence through open invitations.

Though the creation of new songs was a goal of the workshops, I was more interested in creating composers who could continue to make contextually relevant worship music beyond the workshop itself. I pilot-tested these adaptations with two workshops at the end of 2013, then re-initiated monthly "composer's clubs" in 2014. I facilitated three clubs, then transitioned the ongoing leadership of the monthly event to Família Vitoriosa's (VFC) pastor.

I acquired permission to use VFC's sanctuary each fourth Saturday of the month (from 9 a.m. to 12 p.m.) to meet with worship leaders, pastors, and youth. VFC is centrally located and easily accessible by *chapa*.

---

10. King, *Pathways in Christian Music*; Higashi, "Musical Communitas"; Scott, *Moving Into African Music*.

It is known for its worship training events, and is considered safe and neutral territory by pastors (an important consideration for sending *jovens* for training).

In consultation with research assistants, we agreed upon a format that included corporate worship, group discussion, and training on salient topics, and time to compose and develop new worship music. I sent invitations (via cell phone text, a typical means of mass communication) to all the pastors and worship leaders affiliated with the research and to other pastors, musicians, and missionaries I thought might be interested in the event. Table 8 below shows the date of the composer's club session, the number of participants, churches represented, and new songs created.

Table 8: Composer's Clubs Demographics

Session	Participants	Churches	Songs
Oct 2013	30+	7	4
Nov 2013	20	6	4 (2 new)
Feb 2014	28	11	0
Mar 2014	28	9	4
Apr 2014	27	9	3

Pilot Testing Composer's Clubs

During the first meeting, over thirty participants attended, representing seven different churches. After a time of worship, I asked the participants to sketch how they pictured worship,[11] which moved us into a discussion about the definition of worship. We then broke into four groups, purposefully mixing the various churches represented so that they could get to know new people and benefit from multiple viewpoints.

Thankfully, the four groups also had a fairly even distribution of experienced composers who had worked with me in prior songwriting workshops. While this distribution wasn't intentional, it quickly became evident that it was a key factor in successful composition in a short amount of time. In just over an hour, four new songs about peace were

---

11. Witvliet suggests this as a first-day exercise in his chapter entitled, "Teaching Worship as a Christian Practice" ("Teaching Worship," 128).

created, ranging in styles from *nossa música*, to bossa nova with a rap interlude to contemporary soft-rock.

It was raining the day of our second meeting, which affected the number of participants.[12] In addition, there was some confusion as to the date, fourth Saturday is not always the last Saturday of the month. Regardless, twenty participants from five churches attended (almost half had participated in the first meeting). After a concise review of the discussion from the first meeting, I taught about the role of music in worship.

I briefly detailed how to analyze song lyrics, and suggested that the participants consider trying to coordinate the songs with the sermon topic. I also showed the video clips of the songs from the first meeting. We then broke into four groups, two groups further developing two of the peace songs created during the first meeting in an attempt to bring them to completion, and two groups creating Christmas songs. As these groups were also divided by gender, the women's group created a melody for the "Song of Mary" (Luke 1:46–55), while the men's group created a melody for "Zechariah's Song" (Luke 1:68–79).

These first two composer's club sessions pilot tested the songwriting workshop methodology in context. A number of insights were gained from these initial meetings. Monthly sessions, as opposed to a one-time workshop in each church context, seemed to be an important means of not only developing a sense of community, but also momentum and long-term sustainability. This was especially important as there was quite a bit of participant turnover between one session and the next, and the songs were not developing to full maturity for use within church services. Though a core group began to emerge, I prepared each session as a single unit to best reach new and continuing participants.

I also made a point to personally call key musicians and worship leaders, to encourage them and continue to enlist their help in leading composing groups. Their experience and leadership energized the creative process and encouraged the participation of others. Investing in these natural leaders will have effects far beyond a year's worth of composer's clubs. It is my hope that they will take greater ownership of these events, to the point of leading them and continuing beyond the scope of this research.

---

12. It is very difficult to catch a *chapa* when it is raining in Beira—and no one likes to get wet, preferring to wait out the storm.

Composer's Clubs Applied

Our third session was the first composer's club of 2014. Having had a two-month break, I knew a special effort at marketing was needed to reinitiate momentum. I therefore purchased a small radio spot on the local Christian radio station, and twenty-eight participants from eleven churches turned out.

After an initial session of praise and worship and brainstorming new teaching topics together, I taught content analysis methodology, passing out blank tables for each church group to analyze and rank five songs sung in their church context. Rich theological reflection followed, with comments from club participants like, "I don't think this is a wise song to sing in church because it doesn't teach the truth about suffering."[13]

I also taught about the importance of song themes and functions. We then divided into four groups and played a game in which I asked them to sing songs that had various functions (exhortation, worship, proclamation, prayer). I then asked them to sing songs with different themes (baptism, holiness, love, peace, unity, obedience, grace, crucifixion, faith). These games seemed to solidify people's understanding; it was entertaining to watch how people responded (pastors included) to the pressure of competition.

As we only had forty-five minutes left, I simply assigned a gospel book to each group, and asked them to review the last week of Jesus' life and death as Easter was fast approaching. Each group gave a summary report of what they had discovered about the unique perspective of their gospel writer.

Easter was three weeks away by our fourth session, and I was hoping to spend more time composing. However, rain once again impeded our start time and initially participant numbers were low. I made use of the time with a smaller group to tailor a teaching discussion to address their specific concerns and ministry challenges. We talked about how to develop a worship set, what the difference between praise and worship is, and the importance of hospitality in worship.

Once there was a critical mass of people (twenty-eight participants, nine churches), I divided participants up into groups and had them come up with a "mini-service" around a theme (baptism, child dedication, Christmas, Easter) and a simple liturgy format (welcome, two songs, testimony, song, sermon, offering, announcements, exit).

---

13. Meyers, field notes, 2013–14.

Before we moved on to composing, I solicited feedback asking what people had learned. Comments included:[14]

- Everyone has to work together to organize a service.
- You can have a service in just a few minutes, it doesn't take hours.
- The worship team is involved in more than just singing.
- We can organize a service around a theme and this will really help grow the church.

Though the "mini-service" exercise had taken time, it seemed to be worth the effort. In their same groups, they then had a text to work from to compose an Easter song:

1. Triumphal Entry (Matt 21:1–11)
2. Community and Service (John 13:1–20)
3. Crucifixion (Mark 15:33–9)
4. Lord's Supper (Luke 22:14–30)

The resultant songs demonstrated that participants who had attended multiple times were starting to learn the art of composing; the creation process was happening faster with greater musicality and more complete songs that had theological depth and richness.

Two research assistants (both gifted musicians and composers) strongly encouraged me to get some people together to finish the new songs created in composer's clubs. The emphasis on training limited the development and completion of songs. Recognizing that the "starter songs" would not be used until they were completed (defeating one of the purposes of the composer's clubs), I asked them if they would be willing to take on a project to finish the "starter songs," which they agreed to do.

The final composer's club I facilitated before I left the research context was one of transition, passing the baton of leadership on to Pastor João, a musician and gifted teacher, dedicated to growing disciples through worship. After a brief devotional based on Ps 40:3, I reviewed the basics of the songwriting workshop methodology. We discussed what the major concerns of participants' communities were, and the topics gathered included unity, fear of curses, how to behave as a believer, marital

---

14. Ibid.

strife, conflict between parents and children, and how believers should handle ancestor ceremonies.

Twenty-seven participants from nine different churches voted to choose three topics, and then three groups were each assigned a topic. The groups found Bible passages that related to the topic, and then began to compose songs. Three new songs addressing key areas of faith in Mozambique were initiated.

SUMMARY

This applied experimental phase of the research expanded the songwriting workshop model, contextualized for adaptive and sustainable change. Focus group interviews, jam sessions, a voice-technique class, a worship leaders' small-group, and composer's clubs: all these experimental activities initiated change through worship praxis over the course of 2014. Aside from the focus groups and the class, all the other initiatives were ongoing, regular activities that started in February 2014 and continued in my absence from the research context from May to August 2014. Chapter 7 chronicles what happened as a result of these applied activities, answering the question, "How did contextualized worship arts affect church ministry and mission?"

7

Results Assessment: What Happened?

The sanctuary is packed with young people from various denominations who have come to a monthly *Concerto Gileade* (Gilead Concert) hosted by an urban church committed to using the arts to reach and raise young disciples. They are completely riveted to the dramatic presentation, some standing so they can see better, others taking videos with their cell phones.

The actors are portraying a scene in which a worship leader and his drunk friend have gone to a *curandeiro* (witch doctor) in search of peace, but have only succeeded in getting "fleeced." The friends begin to fight, but a pastor intervenes saying, "True peace can only be found in Christ!" Whistles, laughter, shouts, and applause burst forth from the audience.[1]

MY GOAL IN THIS chapter is to describe my findings of how the use of contextualized worship arts in Beira churches have affected church ministry and missions. From the outset it seemed an impossible task to somehow measure the effects of implemented change, particularly within a limited time frame. However, regular and intentional follow-up on the impact of adaptive change is critical to the success of ongoing transformation.

Heifetz suggests that a leader should create a threshold for ongoing involvement by making observations, asking questions, and offering

1. Meyers, Família Vitoriosa (VFC) music event, field notes, 2014–15.

interpretations and intentional actions. "Issues should be internalized, owned and resolved by relevant parties to achieve enduring progress."[2] So, here I offer the reader a "peek" into what is happening in Beira churches today, sharing observations and data collected after the interventions were completed (focus group interviews, numerous training opportunities in holding environments, and composer's clubs).

As in each phase of this research, data for Phase IV was collected by methods triangulation: a simple questionnaire; interviews with pastors, worship leaders, and research partners; and participant observation at various rehearsals, church services, and other events. Below is the research corpus for my final research phase gathered from September to October 2014:

1. Participant Observation: 2 music events, 2 rehearsals, 5 services (at 3 different churches), 2 jam sessions, 1 composer's club, 2 classes at IBS
2. Interviews: 6 pastors, 3 research partners, 10 worship leaders
3. Self-Administered Questionnaire: 40 participants

METHODS APPLIED

I consider the application of each method below, before moving to join the data to Titon's music-performance model.

Self-Administered Questionnaire

Having approximately a month with which to collect data in Phase IV, I knew I could not afford the time to visit each church again, nor interview each pastor. I felt that a self-administered questionnaire would allow me to gather data from a large representative sample (40 responses) at various events and activities without the worry of interviewer bias and response effects. Each survey participant had been involved in some type of change process activity. I approached every respondent individually and asked if they would be willing to fill out a questionnaire about the research activities and return it to me (drop and collect method). Completion usually took five to ten minutes. In some cases I asked the questions and wrote down the answers, but the majority of responses were completed autonomously. I was present during the time of completion

---

2. Heifetz and Linsky, *Leadership On the Line*, 1959.

and available to participants for follow-up clarification. The questioning route was as follows:

1. Participant information (gender, church, number of clubs or other activities)
2. What are you doing in music/worship since the composer's club or other activities?
3. How did these clubs and/or other activities contribute to music/worship (personally, in your church, in the community outside the church)?

The overarching purpose of the questionnaire was to discover how the expanded songwriting workshop model (that is, the composer's clubs, jam sessions, worship leaders' small groups and classes) impacted participants.

Interviews

Three types of interviews were administered to three sets of people. Each interview had a separate questioning route. I interviewed six pastors using the following questions:

1. What are you thinking about worship in your church today?
2. Has the work that I've done contributed in some way to the vision God has given you?
3. Could we do better? What's missing?

My goal in these interviews was to ascertain impact inside the local church, whether pastors were indeed drawing on the multiple training opportunities to shape their congregations.

My second set of interviews was designed for my three research partners, the men who sustained change process activities (jam sessions, composer's clubs, and worship leaders' small groups) in my four-month absence from the research context. I asked them the questions below:

1. Describe the process of "giving back the work." How was it for you while I was away?
2. What could I have done differently or better to empower you to lead?

106　Part Three: Grazing and Growing

    3. What do you want to do going forward? How is God leading you now?

These interviews helped me gain a better understanding of what happened while I was not present, allowed me to reconnect with my research partners, and to learn how best to move forward in research and ministry. They also enabled me to document how I had given back the work and mentored others.

The last set of interviews was informal conversations with worship leaders who had shown particular interest and engagement prior to my departure. In these ten cases, the questioning route varied from person to person. I used the self-administered questionnaire as a springboard for deeper conversations, probing for more details, and clarifying certain answers to get a more holistic understanding of the impact of the change process on their lives and ministry.

Participant Observation

In this last phase of my research, I once again used participant observation as a means of data collection. My goal was to observe as many music events in as many different locations as I could within a month, to see with my own eyes what was happening in Beira, rather than hearing about it second hand. Field notes include two music events and two worship team rehearsals at Família Vitoriosa (VFC), five services at three different churches, two roots jam meetings, one composer's club and two classes at Instituto Bíblico de Sofala (IBS). I wanted to verify that the additional activities did, in fact, enhance capacity among musicians and leaders and engender greater engagement as witnessed in multiple music events.

Having outlined the methods used in this final phase of research, I move to present my questionnaire findings that substantiate a positive correlation between an expanded songwriting workshop model and enhanced culturally appropriate worship in the local churches of Beira.

CULTURALLY APPROPRIATE WORSHIP ENHANCED: QUESTIONNAIRE FINDINGS

The questionnaire was specifically designed to determine the effects of the expanded model, that is, the additional change process activities, as experienced by the participants. Appendix G shows the survey results.

Seventy-eight percent of the participants were male, typical of a patriarchal society and clearly evident in church leadership and worship praxis. Thirteen denominations were represented, though only seven were part of the initial study. This indicates that the impact of the change process extends beyond the cases researched.

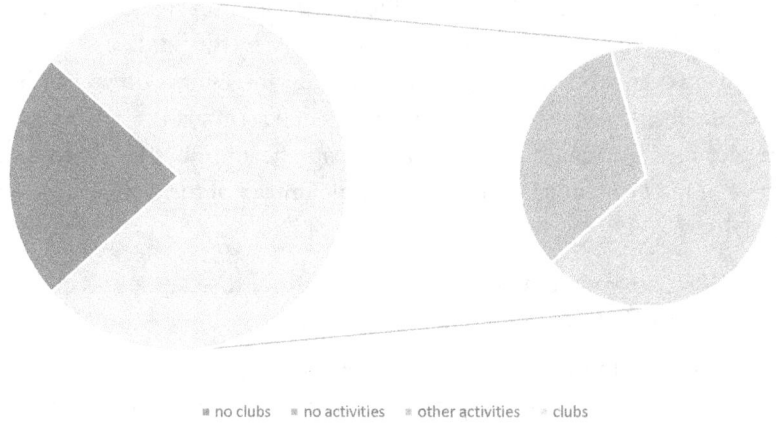

■ no clubs   ■ no activities   ■ other activities   ■ clubs

Figure 10: Participation in Change Process Activities

Each participant had engaged in some sort of change process activity, composer's club, jam session, worship leaders' small group, or class. Figure 10 shows that 70 percent of the forty respondents participated in composer's clubs (light grey), while 30 percent of the respondents did not (dark grey). Of the twenty-eight respondents that did participate in composer's clubs, 68 percent were involved in other activities (light medium grey), while 32 percent were not (medium grey).

One of my central research concerns was to discover ways to expand the capacity of the songwriting workshop model for enhancing culturally appropriate worship in the local church. I therefore needed to first expand the capacity of the model. I accomplished this through focus groups and the change process activities indicated above. The focus of the fourth phase of the research, then, was to discover if these alterations to the songwriting workshop model did, in fact, enhance culturally appropriate worship. Was there a noticeable difference between the responses of those who had attended only composer's clubs versus those who also partook in other activities?

In comparing responses of those who had participated in other activities versus clubs alone (see Appendix G), the only distinguishing factor was the church, the majority of the questionnaire respondents who only attended composer's clubs were from Família Vitoriosa (VFC). Responses to the second and third questions were remarkably similar. In fact, even for those participants that did not attend any clubs, the impact of other activities was analogous. Therefore, the impact of the expanded songwriting workshop model alone was not substantiated by this study.

However, while the data collected does not show a difference between clubs versus other activities, the evidence of a collective positive impact on individuals and churches is significant. Questions two and three of the questionnaire honed in on the impact of the change process activities:

- What are you doing in music/worship since the composer's club or other activities?
- How did these clubs and/or other activities contribute to music/worship (personally, in your church, in the community outside the church)?

A thematic analysis of the responses to these questions revealed three distinct domains, or taxonomies of positive influence: personal, corporate, and innovation. Seventy-three percent of respondents designated multiple domains, creating overlapping circles of impact (see figure 11). Let us look at each in turn.

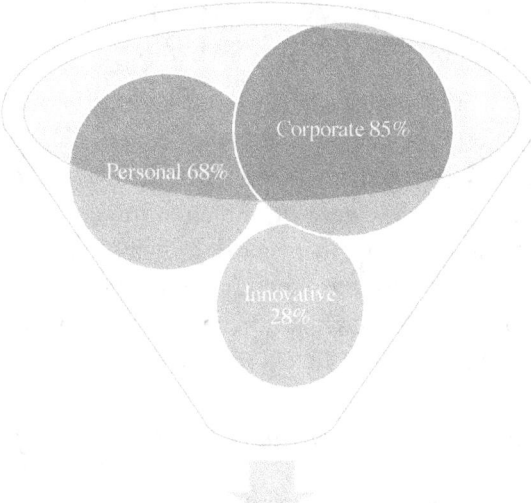

New Worship Praxis

Figure 11: Impact of Change Process Activities

The personal domain arena includes words like "learning, practicing, growing, and using," showing that respondents are applying the activities personally. Sixty-eight percent of participants indicated that the activities influenced them on a personal level. The corporate domain takes it a step further, with words such as "teaching, leading, shaping, helping, preaching, and ministering." These words involve influencing others. Eighty-five percent of respondents denoted influence in a corporate reality. Finally, the innovation domain, with words like "composing or creating," imply change and formation of new ideas and behavior patterns in church ministry and missions. Twenty-eight percent of respondents specified this last domain.

Each of these domains separately and together denote the emergence of new worship praxis in Beira churches in and beyond the cases studied. In comparison with research gathered in Phase II (see chapters 4 and 5), it is clear that the change process activities, both the composer's clubs and the other activities, positively contributed to the development of church ministry and mission, enhancing culturally appropriate worship in the local church.

MUSIC-PERFORMANCE MODEL APPLIED TO CHANGE RESULTS: DATA ANALYSIS

Questionnaire results indicated that the experimental methods had a positive impact on local churches. However, data was also gleaned from participant observation and interviews. What did these other data sources indicate about the development of church ministry and mission in Beira? Titon's music-performance model, having served as a framework throughout this study, also proved useful in describing the multilayered components of change occurring in Beira churches noted through data collection from September to October 2014.

Time and Space, Increased Use of Contextual Worship Arts

> The day of the concert, Beira stopped. I cried, and thought, "It's really happening, this is something Beira really needs. It was worth it!"[3]

One Saturday in July of 2014, approximately five hundred people, representing over thirty church denominations from all over the central region of Mozambique, came to Beira for a gospel concert held at an old movie theater. Many pastors canceled their other Saturday events, encouraging their congregants to participate in the concert. The band, dressed in African clothes, played only locally composed songs. People are still talking about how wonderful the concert was, and the need for another concert soon. This event happened while I was in the United States.

---

3. Meyers, Manuel Mário, field notes, 2014–15.

Results Assessment: What Happened? 111

Figure 12: Beira Gospel Concert

What changes took place in Beira from January to July 2014 in order for a concert of this magnitude to happen? What change effects on time and space does this concert indicate, and how did this study contribute to the outcome of a citywide interdenominational gospel concert?

There are certainly numerous factors involved far beyond the scope of this study, up to and including a movement of the Holy Spirit, which none of us can claim but in which all of us can cooperate. The Lord went ahead of this research, inspiring other music events during 2014 such as a citywide gospel choir competition, numerous new Christian CDs, and other Christian concerts.

These activities, or confounding variables, were not anticipated prior to the creation of Phase III, applying adaptive change, yet they contributed to the overall sense of growing enthusiasm for Mozambican worship in Beira. It is certain that these events impacted the rate and level of change in worship praxis in the churches studied. Beira was "ripe" for change, and I was grateful to be able to conduct research during this pivotal phase in worship history in Beira, recording a story of transformation through music.

But beyond a growing consensus at large, were there any change components that contributed to the creation of this concert? Can we draw any accurate conclusions as to the impact of the experimental interventions on local churches? Manuel Mário, the concert producer, stated:

> This concert wouldn't have existed without the composer's clubs, worship leaders' small group and jam sessions. These other groups provided a network of people with similar vision and training from which to draw upon to organize the concert. I've organized other events like this in Beira before, but this time it was different, it was easier.[4]

Numerous one-on-one conversations with Manuel, trusting relationships with pastors built over the course of this research, and multiple events where worship leaders and musicians were challenged about the importance of contextualized worship arts all helped to ripen the Christian community to embrace this new initiative.

There is a groundswell of developing Christian artists who are producing concerts, CDs, and videos in Beira. There were at least four CD projects in the making the month I returned to the city (September 2014), music projects that are distinctly Mozambican. One youth said, "I've realized I need to change, to be more contextual in my music. My music was Western. I'm learning to create Mozambican music now."[5] Youth are starting to embrace Mozambican culture, demonstrated by a marked difference in the number of young people wearing African clothes from previous years. Yet this is a hybrid fashion trend, African cloth with Western design patterns. This indicates that youth are beginning to realize the value of cultural traditions, but they are reappropriating traditions for themselves.

Though not all churches are this welcoming, VFC is now hosting a monthly *Concerto Gileade* in which new artists can share their art with peers in a nonthreatening environment. These concerts, usually drawing a crowd of 150–200 young people from numerous city churches, "are a direct result of this study's efforts," according to Helder Andrade, a worship leader at VFC.[6] The weight of a noncontextualized gospel mission history is lifting. Mozambicans in Beira are celebrating, praising God in new forms that are contextually relevant, but biblically solid.

---

4. Meyers, field notes, 2014–15.
5. Ibid.
6. Ibid.

Audience and Community, Engaged Pastors, Empowered Worship Leaders

> We're talking about worship at our general conference. There's a motivation to change among leadership, it's not just me.[7]

Increased use of contextualized arts in Beira is evident, but what about the rift in relationships between pastors and youth? How has this study impacted a social hierarchy that robs young worship leaders of the authority to lead worship, and diminishes the importance of worship in the eyes of the congregation?

Pastor João of Família Vitoriosa (VFC) is probably one of the best examples of an engaged pastor, one who has caught the vision of this research and has really moved his church in a new direction. The day after the focus group discussion at VFC, he completely disbanded the worship team, realizing that there were deep issues that needed addressing before the team would be ready to minister. He attended each worship rehearsal for a year, and was intimately involved in training worship leaders, analyzing song lyrics, and composing new songs.

Pastor Adriano of Aurora Messiânica (AM) is also actively participating in the change process at his church. He asked for help in creating a liturgy that combines traditional hymns with contemporary worship, disclosing, "We still need to figure out an adequate way to address our worship wars."[8] He managed to get worship on the agenda for the denomination's general conference in December 2015, and asked for training (for himself and other worship leaders) specifically related to liturgy, addressing how to create a service that respects both types of musical preferences present in his church and that builds unity in the body.

Pastor Nyazeze of Nova Aliança (NA) is a provincial pastor, in charge of all of the NA churches in Sofala. Though he has great responsibility, his influence is limited. "I've been a part of the district leadership, but I can't do anything in a local context without the other leader's support."[9] He admitted to me that the conversations we've had have impacted him. "They contributed to help me think and reflect about what is

---

7. Meyers, Pastor Adriano, field notes, 2014–15.
8. Meyers, field notes, 2014–15.
9. Ibid.

praise and worship in our churches. It really helped me personally to pay attention to the words, to what we're doing and why."[10]

In our last conversation, Nyazeze informed me that the denomination had just received a large tract of land in Manga (a neighboring town to Beira). He'd been tasked to create a training school and model church for other NA churches. Pastor Nyazeze is seventy-two, yet at the twilight of his life he is still passionate about training church leadership and raising up the next generation. "Now I can start a church service with quality, the way worship should be. It may be easier than trying to evolve a pre-existing mature church."[11]

Not all pastors are as excited about worship as Nyazeze or João. However, at the very least, they are now aware of the importance of worship, the need for further training and development, and they are asking for more support. My 2014 worship class at Instituto Bíblico de Sofala (IBS) doubled in size from 2013, many students being financially supported by their churches. Pastor Arão said, "It was a short time. To learn good things takes time. The seeds have been planted, they've germinated, now they just need some more watering."[12] Though the generational rift still exists in churches, it is clear that, in some cases studied, the change components contributed profoundly in engaging pastors and leadership in process transformation through worship.

Performers and Performance, Intentional Use of Worship for Teaching

> During our conference, we chose songs that were related to the conference themes, or connected to the sermon topic. This really helped learning; people left singing the songs and taking the ideas home.[13]

There are unmistakable signs of growth involving pastors and leadership with worship in the local church. Yet, how has the change process impacted the music-performance itself? Research revealed that a fractured rather than cohesive service is common in worship services, that sermons

---

10. Ibid.
11. Ibid.
12. Ibid.
13. Meyers, Pastor João, field notes, 2014–15.

and songs are rarely organized thematically. How did the training events impact liturgy?

A more concerted effort to intentionally plan services is evident. Norse, the worship group leader from First Baptist Church, informed me that the team now meets right after Sunday services to plan the next week's songs. They spend the week in prayer and reflection about the songs so that they are prepared for rehearsal on Saturday.

Another shift at First Baptist is a rotation between the women's choir and the praise team. Last year, the two groups would vary leading throughout the service. As the groups were not planning worship together, each group would sing their own songs that had diverse themes, resulting in a fragmented music event. Now the groups take turns leading the entire service allowing for a more unified thematic musical performance.

Família Vitoriosa (VCF) has also taken the notion of teaching through music seriously. Each song must go through a rigorous analysis: Is it biblical? Is it culturally relevant? Is it consistent with church doctrine? If a song does not pass muster, it is not performed during the worship service. Pastor João is committed to making sure that there is no conflict between the spoken and the sung Word.

The intentional use of music to teach theological principles is a growth edge for the Mozambican church. Some pastors specifically mentioned this point as an area of weakness. Pastor Nyazeze said, "I think people are mixed up, invoking Jesus and his blood or the Holy Spirit, but also calling Satan and his actions. Some songs still don't have biblical content."[14] The Pentecostal heritage of "let the spirit lead" combined with an allergy to Catholicism are still barriers to an interrelated liturgy.

Yet, there is a hunger for more instruction in how to select and place songs. This continues to be a popular teaching topic at workshops and conferences. When I asked two worship leaders what kind of hymnal would be most practical for use in local churches, their immediate response was to create a hymnal with songs organized into liturgical categories including: Hearing the Word, Confessing our Faith, and Living our Faith. Concerted efforts to create a cohesive thematic music performance can contribute in clarifying biblical principles and cementing them in the minds and hearts of believers.

---

14. Meyers, field notes, 2014–15.

Music and Affective Experience: Growing Corpus of Indigenous Hymnody

> If you stop (doing composer's clubs) VFC will continue. We are already seeing the fruits; songs are more biblical and more connected to this cultural context.[15]

The music-performance of worship in Beira churches is starting to shift toward a more unified thematic presentation. What about the songs themselves? Are the new songs created in composer's clubs being used in churches? Are unbiblical songs still sung?

Three pastors expressed grave concern in this last set of interviews that their congregations are singing songs that aren't appropriate, "We are singing songs that have superficial content."[16] As stated above, another pastor articulated the presence of lyric syncretism, calling both God and Satan. Two of these three pastors, however, do not have direct leadership over a local church, so their influence on song selection during a church service is limited.

The other three pastors interviewed have intentionally eliminated all songs from the church repertoire that have unbiblical or confusing content. In the case of Família Vitoriosa (VFC), composing new songs still continues. Their goal in 2014 was to sing a majority of locally composed songs within a year's time. They are well on their way to reaching this goal, as exemplified on September 28, 2014, when three new VFC songs were sung in a five-song set. This was a remarkable achievement.

RELATIONSHIPS ARE EVERYTHING

Having explored each arena of Titon's music-performance model individually, I once again "zoom out" to make some final remarks about the project as a whole. In this section, my goal is to examine additional factors (confounding variables) that influenced the success of the research, namely the level of impact the change process methodology had on the twelve cases studied. In Table 9 I demonstrate which churches engaged in which activities during the course of the research.

Table 9 demonstrates that I was unable to garner full participation by all twelve churches throughout each phase of the research. As American Board (AB) and Assembleia de Deus Africana (ADA) joined the research at the end of Phase II, I was unable to collect sufficient baseline data,

---

15. Meyers, Pastor João, field notes, 2014–15.
16. Meyers, field notes, 2014–15.

rendering their case data null for experimental analysis. In Phase IV, I was also unable to follow-up with representatives from União Baptista (UB), therefore voiding UB. Of the remaining ten cases, Nova Alliança (NA) inadvertently became my control for Phase III, as I was unable to conduct a focus group interview and no one from NA attended any of the training opportunities offered. This unexpected outcome, included in my multiple baseline experimental design for Phase III, helped to control for confounding variables in analysis. The question follows, then, was there a discernible difference between the outcomes of the other nine churches and NA?

Table 9: Church Participation in Research Phases

Phases:	I			II					III	
Church	P/O	Int	C/A	CC	FG	IL	RJ	Class	F/U	Total:
1stB	X	X	X	X	X	X	X	X	X	9
VPD	X	X	X	X	X	X	X	X	X	9
UB	X	X	X		X	X				5
NA	X	X	X						X	4
ECD	X	X	X	X	X	X	X	X	X	9
ADA	X	X		(X)					X	4
ADI	X	X	X	X		X		X	X	7
ADE	X	X		X	X				X	5
MEVN	X	X	X	X	X		X		X	7
AM	X	X	X	X	X				X	6
AB	X				X	X				3
VFC	X	X	X	X	X	X	X	X	X	9
Total:	12	11	9	8	10	7	5	5	10	

Key: P/O: Participant Observation at Church Service; Int: Structured Interview with Pastor; C/A: Content Analysis; CC: Composer's Club; FG: Focus Group; IL: Internato Levítico (Worship Leader's Small Group); RJ: Roots Jam; F/U: Follow-up (questionnaire, interview or participant observation)

Thankfully, I was able to conduct a follow-up interview with Pastor Nyazeze of NA and compare his responses to those of five other pastors whose churches participated in Phase III (see Appendix H). My purpose in these interviews was to discover the impact of the Phase III interventions inside the local church. As mentioned above, my questioning route included:

1. What are you thinking about worship in your church today?
2. Has the work that I've done contributed in some way to the vision God has given you?
3. Could we do better? What is missing?

Each pastor indicated varying degrees of positive change in their local congregations, with the exception of Pastor Nyazeze (NA). Though he was quick to reassure me that he'd been personally challenged to think critically about how churches are worshipping, and asked for my input in developing a worship curriculum, he also expressed deep concern about syncretism in worship at NA. His response validates the claim that the experimental interventions conducted in Phase III had a positive impact on worship praxis in the other nine participating churches.

Though my goal throughout the study was certainly to include all cases in each phase of research, considerable obstacles prevented total participation, primarily distance (from church site), and other church commitments. For example, though the Aurora Messiânica's (AM) pastor was very engaged in this project, the church is quite far from the city center, and finding transportation to and from events was difficult. Nova Alliança (NA) and União Baptista (UB) were both participants in the gospel choir competition, held at the beginning of 2014. This meant that potential participants in change process activities were already occupied with other musical events and responsibilities. However, participation in each phase of research was not the only indicator of worship transformation in local churches.

Another critical component of effective change was related to relationships, with whom I was interacting, and how they were viewed in the church community. The participant's roles and responsibilities in the local congregation determined the level of influence. Pastor Nhazeze of NA is part of the provincial leadership, but not directly responsible for leading a local congregation. Therefore, while he personally was invested in the research, the impact on NA was not significant. This also holds true for Assembleia de Deus Africana (ADA), Assembleia de Deus Internacional (ADI), and Primeira Igreja Baptista (1stB), where my pastoral contact is responsible for multiple churches, but not directly in control of a local congregation.

In other cases, local pastors, though they expressed interest in the project, had previous agendas and priorities that impeded the research process. This was certainly discouraging, but an inevitable part of the mess of qualitative research. Certainly the level of trust established in my relationship with them played a role. Generally speaking, those pastors with whom I had the least affinity also proved to be the most problematic. The relationship between researcher and subject is a key element in the success of applied research.

Since "worship leader" as a category is ambiguous in Beira, finding the de facto music leader was also challenging. Some worship leaders have the title but not the capacity or influence to bring about change, as in the case of Visão na Palavra de Deus (VPD), Evangelho Completo de Deus (ECD), Missão Evangélica de Vida Nova (MEVN), and Primeira Igreja Baptista (1stB). In these cases, though they all participated in each phase of the research, the change results were disappointing.

A final factor in the level of success was the denominational structure itself. Família Vitoriosa (VFC), whose structure is minimal and flexible, had the ability to affect radical change in a short time span. Pastor Arão, retired pastor of 1stB, on the other hand, was still hoping to gain permission to get the idea of a worship pastor on the agenda for a December 2014 meeting in our October interview. Change, particularly in churches with entrenched hierarchical structures, takes more time than a few months to occur.

When one combines all the above factors, it is easy to see why Família Vitoriosa (VFC) experienced the most transformation over the course of the research. As VFC was my primary case site, it was involved in each phase of the research. In fact, it was my experiences at VFC and with Pastor João that inspired me to begin this research in the first place. We had worked together for two years prior to beginning the research, and the relationship was solid. He opened the door to the church, and to the worship ministry, shared honestly about the challenges in ministry and mission, and fully cooperated each step along the way.

Because I had so much prior exposure to Família Vitoriosa (VFC), I was also more aware of the political climate, particularly in relation to leadership and the worship team. I knew the relational dynamics between team members, who had capacity and influence and who did not, and I spent more time at VFC than at any other church. This built trust which, in turn, created an openness to learn and grow. Once, when asking Pastor João permission to reinitiate composer's clubs, he looked at me and said, "Why are you asking me? You are at home here. Be free."[17] In other words, my long-term relationship with VFC gave me a unique research advantage that I did not have in other churches. I could effectively focus my efforts and initiate change because I knew the church well. Relationships are everything.

SUMMARY

In this chapter I have described my findings of how the intentional use of contextualized worship arts in Beira churches has affected church ministry and missions. I demonstrated how the expanded songwriting workshop model enhanced culturally appropriate worship in local churches. Using Titon's music-performance model as a rubric, I also confirmed an increased use of contextualized worship arts, engaged pastors and empowered worship leaders, intentional use of worship to teach, and a growing corpus of indigenous hymnody. Lastly, I explored overarching factors beyond the research itself that influenced the effectiveness of the change process activities, showing that a long-term relationship with a church was essential.

In this following conclusion, I demonstrate the necessity of contextualized worship arts as a key component of the development of the local church and its members, encouraging personal discipleship, growing ministry, and empowering for mission.

---

17. Meyers, field notes, 2014–2015.

CONCLUSION

Grazing, Growing, and Going

I FINALLY COME TO the big picture question, "So what?" What is the importance of this contextually applied research for the Mozambican church? What are the lessons learned and the following implications for the development of church ministry and mission through music?

FOUR-ARENA APPROACH TO ETHNODOXOLOGY REVISITED: INSIDE-OUT

Throughout this study I have used Titon's music-performance model as a rubric to discuss various aspects of the worship reality in Beira.[1] King's four-arena approach to ethnomusicology-in-mission also utilizes four overlapping circles to describe how music in culture impacts the biblical text, music makers and personal pilgrimage, the faith community, and the missional context shown in figure 13.[2]

---

1. Titon, *Worlds of Music*, 11.
2. King, *Music in the Life*, 13.

122 Conclusion: Grazing, Growing, and Going

                    Music in Culture & the
                        Missional Context

Music in   Music in
Culture &   Culture &
the Faith   the Biblical
Community   Text

                      Music Makers &
                      Personal Pigrimage

Figure 13: Four-Arena Approach to Ethnomusicology-in-Mission[3]

If one merges the two models (see figure 14), one gets a sense not only of the holistic nature of ethnodoxology,[4] but also the ever expanding nature and influence (like a pebble in a pond) of the biblical text in music (scripture songs) on performers and their personal pilgrimage, the audience (faith community), and on the missional context outside of the church. The greater the scripture song, the greater the impact. If the whole gospel is not sung, it affects not just the performers or the audience but the entire music culture.

---

3. Permission grated by Baylor University Press to reuse the figure "A Matrix for Studies in Global Church Music (Studies in Ethnomusicology and the Christian Faith)," from King, *Music in the Life of the African Church* with modifications as shown above.

4. I prefer to use the term "ethnodoxology" rather than "ethnomusicology in mission" purely for efficiency's sake as I feel the terms are interchangeable. Ethnodoxology links worship and mission, and includes multiple art forms; it is more than just music.

Conclusion: Grazing, Growing, and Going 123

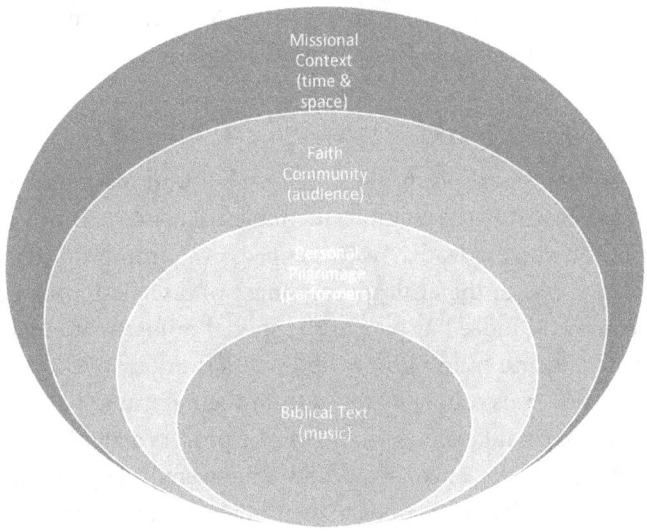

Figure 14: Missiological Implications of Contextual Worship Arts

Conversely, as I have argued in chapter 5, the surrounding missional context, the audience and community, and the performers, influence the music itself. There is an ongoing musical dialectic between content and context.

What does this look like in Beira? How do contextual worship arts impact musicians, congregations, and the world outside the four walls of the church? How can musicians graze on the Word of God, grow in their knowledge of Him, and then go share their songs of faith with others? I apply the hybrid model (figure 14) to the church context in Beira, Mozambique, this time going from the inside out.

Biblical Text (Music and Affective Experience)

How does the church in Beira interact with the Scriptures? What theology is revealed in the songs sung each Sunday? As mentioned in chapter 5, content analysis of frequently sung songs revealed a fragile faith and an incomplete gospel: strong proclamation and praise on Sunday, but little teaching on a life of discipleship from Monday to Saturday. Yet discussions with my research assistants and songwriting workshop participants disclosed incredible self-theologizing capabilities. Ongoing composer's clubs began to instill a passion for studying the Bible and creating new scripture songs for the discipleship of the church body in Beira. As these songs were incorporated into the sung repertoire of the church, people began to graze and grow in God's Word through song.

Personal Pilgrimage (Performers and Performance)

This dimension looks specifically at the people who make and minister through music within the cultural and missional context. The discouraging stories of worship leaders who stepped away from ministry due to immorality spoke to the critical component of discipleship as a part of this research and indeed as part of the special ministry of ethnodoxology. Mentoring and training worship leaders is imperative not only for growth in their musical ability but also in their spiritual practices, and became an important element in the change process activities. As young worship leaders were encouraged and empowered, they continued to grow as leaders and as worshippers; their influence among their peers, in their local congregations, and in their communities blossomed.

Faith Community (Audience and Community)

In this arena we explore how music actively ministers the gospel to the broader congregation. Participating in worship draws the congregation into a dialogue with the Divine. By praying, praising, and proclaiming God's active presence together, the congregation moves from being an audience to being "a chosen people, a royal priesthood, a holy nation, God's special possession, that you may declare the praises of him who called you out of darkness into his wonderful light" (1 Pet 2:9). Music making is a spiritual discipline, discovering God through an act of faith in worship. However, the missionary legacy has encouraged many Mozambican Christians to become Western in worship, passively grazing in a foreign pasture. Teaching critical contextualization has challenged existing worship practice and engendered the rediscovery of a redeemed identity as a Christian Mozambican, delaying cultural attrition, and deepening a worship practice that feels at home to the next generation of Mozambicans. Beira believers can now graze and grow in their own church fields.

Missional Context (Time and Space)

The missional context is the cultural setting in which a church is placed. What happens when church music is played outside of the church? One friend said, "It was the music, not the preaching, that drew me into the church."[5] Conversions as a result of jam sessions held throughout the city bear witness to music's attractional and transformative qualities, drawing people into relationship with God and the church community. Music is more than just a tool for communication or for marketing, but a means of mission. As one young musician said, "I knew that Christians were supposed to share the gospel with others, but I didn't feel comfortable preaching. Now I know I can share my faith in song!"[6] As Beira believers have been able to graze and grow in their faith through music, they are now going beyond the four walls of the church to sing.

FOR FURTHER RESEARCH

This study, like all studies, had its limitations and weaknesses. Furthermore, it uncovered additional questions and areas for exploration that were beyond the boundaries of this research. Here I would like to address these issues in the hope that someone will build on this study and take it even further.

Using Indigenous Hymnody

One of the strengths of the monthly composer's clubs was also its weakness, that is, the teaching component. While it helped to train composers, it left little time to actually compose songs. This was further exacerbated by a revolving door of participants from multiple churches, some much less musically gifted than others. Though the network of composers was expanded, it made it difficult to gain momentum in creating and developing new hymnody, resulting in only two mature songs that are being used in churches today. In seven composer's clubs over the course of a year, seventeen new scripture songs were initiated that had not fully matured.

In an attempt to foster further implementation, I started working with some worship leaders and musicians to bring the new songs to maturity and to create a hymnal of songs organized around a liturgy. The project will be a collection of both popular worship songs and new scripture songs that are biblically solid and contextually relevant with an accompanying CD. Once completed, I will distribute this resource

---

5. Meyers, field notes, 2012–13.
6. Meyers, field notes, 2013–14.

through ministry networks, seminaries, and local bookstores, as a preliminary measure of disseminating contextualized worship music into the local church context.

Additionally, ad hoc composer's clubs are ongoing at Família Vitoriosa (VFC) at the request of Pastor João. Long-term training, local application, and advocacy from the leadership is making an impact on Sunday liturgy. Upon discovering that the church did not have any offering songs in their repertoire during the September 2014 club, VFC composer's club participants composed an offering song that is still being used. A corollary study exploring the impact of a focused long-term effort to develop composers and indigenous hymnody in one local church is in order.

Engaging Pastors, Empowering Worship Leaders

Due to the limited time and the sheer number of cases involved in this study, deep relationships with pastors and worship leaders in each church was impossible. Greater impact was clearly evident in those cases where the relationships were stronger. Narrative research, chronicling the effects of the change process activities on an individual pastor or worship leader and the resultant change in worship praxis would be fascinating.

I continue to remain committed to mentoring worship leaders and encouraging pastors to engage in worship through various training opportunities, namely through worship classes at local seminaries, worship workshops, and conferences. As relationships grow, so will the influence of changed worship praxis.

Worshipping Faith Communities

Data collection in the fourth phase of research through a questionnaire, interviews, and a self-report did not include an assessment of the impact of the change process activities on the participating congregations. Though certainly the hardest variable to test, a cross-case diachronic study of the influence of new worship praxis on the development of the local church members would make a significant contribution to this research.

Participating as a member at VFC, I witnessed first-hand the faith journey of fellow members as we worshiped together. Informal conversations, shared meals, and Bible studies are all venues for continuing to discover the development of the local faith community of VFC.

Missioning in the Musical Context

Studies exploring the influence of contextualized worship arts in the surrounding cultural context would be a fascinating addition to this research. I had limited access to traditional music culture events and was further limited by time in the research context. Therefore, my study was primarily focused on church contexts. The question remains: how does the use of culturally appropriate worship impact the missional context?

The jam sessions project, an open-air public evangelistic music event, was initiated in order to validate and build competency in the performance of *nossa música* as well as to move Christian musicians beyond the comfort of the four walls of the church. It continues to attract people from multiple denominations who are interested in sharing their faith through song. Musicians publicly performing *nossa música* always draw an audience of people, some curious passersby, some Christians who join in singing along, some who come for prayer. Jam sessions are a powerful means of musical evangelism, going places that Sunday worship services don't reach. Through performance ethnography with this group of musicians, I observe what impact contextual worship arts has on the broader community outside the four walls of the church.

RECOMMENDATIONS FOR EXPANDING ETHNODOXOLOGY PRAXIS

Moving beyond the local church context, I finally consider the implications of this study for the discipline of ethnodoxology, that is, applied ethnomusicology in mission. Here I humbly offer a few lessons learned in the trenches of research.

Lessons Learned

Deep relationships over an extended period of time are absolutely critical to the sustainable success of applied research. Relationships help a researcher understand the context, including power dynamics and songs-in-use. Relationships also give you the information needed to reframe the method to suit the specific context. Finally, relationships enable you to ensure that the changes will stick for the long haul. The incredible transformation of VFC was only possible because of my long-term relationship with the pastor and the church body.

I argue that, in the long run, mentoring musicians is more important than making music. As the Chinese adage goes, "It is better to teach a man to fish than give him a fish." This holds true in ethnodoxology. Though it is tempting to focus on creating music products, in this case scripture songs, it is much more effective in the long run to create music producers.

This has been observed in Ferkessédougou, Côte d'Ivoire, where musicians are now producing their own music. Roberta King initiated songwriting workshops among the Nyarafolo in the early '90s, shortly after one believer began producing songs in his indigenous musical style. After two of these workshops, several song composers began implementing the process on their own: contemplating Scripture truths and stories, and finding a song.

They initiated a couple more workshops on their own, but have realized that the process has taken off as a movement of its own, with the most talented song composers creating many songs and also training others. In the weekly meetings of the Nyarafolo Outreach Group, new songs are practiced monthly and edited by the group, especially as new singers emerge. One villager mentored by the early workshops now often spontaneously composes songs based on messages, singing them at the end of the service.

Empowered musicians, such as those in Côte d'Ivoire, will continue to produce music long after my ministry term is done. While mentoring is time consuming and messy, the impact is exponentially greater. Second Tim 2:2 says, "And the things you have heard me say in the presence of many witnesses entrust to reliable people who will also be qualified to teach others." Let us not get caught up in products and forget the people we have been called to teach.

Pastors are power brokers and key players in the transformation of local church worship praxis. This is particularly true in the authoritarian and patriarchal culture of Mozambique. The churches that experienced the most significant changes in worship were those whose pastors were most fully engaged in the research process. I suspect that this principle also holds true in other contexts as well.

While preserving traditional music culture is important, it may not be people's heart music. Permission to engage traditional music culture in worship was rarely encouraged in Mozambican churches. A noncontextualized missionary legacy, globalization, and urban youth culture have significantly impacted preferred worship styles in Beira churches. Our goal must be to encourage heartfelt worship, creating maximum opportunities for believers to engage God. Heart music can encompass a range of musical styles that can be redeemed as vehicles for God's glory. It is not a matter of simply replacing Western music with local songs. Taking the music people love away from them (even if it is contemporary Christian music from Australia) is a form of neocolonialism.

Worship does not need to be a dualistic either/or phenomenon. Rather, it is a both/and experience, where we graze and grow from a global and local musical menu. Particularly in the urban church context, we must make room at the table for the musical hybridities that are the inevitable result of cocreating and singing together on the pilgrim road.

Collegial Cautions for Ethnodoxologists

Having shared some observations gleaned through research, I now offer some strategies for ethnodoxology best praxis based on this study.

Creating Local Arts Together: A Manual to Help Communities Reach their Kingdom Goals (Schrag and Krabill), is a book designed exclusively to help engage church communities in cocreating contextual worship arts for mission. Methodology includes seven steps:

1. Meet a community and its arts
2. Specify kingdom goals
3. Select effects, content, genre, and events
4. Analyze an event containing the chosen genre
5. Spark creativity
6. Improve new works
7. Integrate and celebrate for continuity

This research in many ways paralleled this approach. I met the twelve church communities and their arts, and gleaned from pastors through structured interviews what their kingdom goals were. Worship music was the chosen genre, and I analyzed multiple music events containing the chosen genre in various church services. I sparked creativity through focus groups, composer's clubs, worship leaders' small groups, roots jams, and classes. Each activity met the needs and interests of different people, the complex whole of these diverse activities contributing to the overall change impact.

Ongoing rehearsals and other opportunities, such as roots jams, gospel concerts, CD projects, and choir competitions, helped to further improve the new works. Finally, these new works are slowly being integrated into regular use in churches as they gain popularity and are shared through a network of musical relationships. My research suggests, however, that there are a few additional components that can significantly contribute to the successful integration and continuation of culturally appropriate worship within and beyond the local church.

First, though the author acknowledges early on that "people are multilingual, multicultural, and multiartistic," the manual does not, in my opinion, sufficiently describe how to understand the complexities of this reality.[7] Particularly in an urban environment like Beira, it is virtually impossible to untangle the threads of varying music traditions, including missional influence, multiple languages, and numerous cultures, that contribute to the music tapestry of worship music in city churches. Ethnodoxologists need to be better equipped to understand the increasingly globalized reality of worship in today's urban churches.

Furthermore, church music is a form of pop music; in other words, a current phenomenon. Schrag's suggestion to "give extra attention to local artists who represent older, geographically or ethnically rooted traditions because their skills and knowledge are of unique value" does not acknowledge the competing ideas and identities brought by globalization that shape worship music.[8] While an attempt to explore traditional music forms is admirable and even necessary, it is not the only arena that needs rigorous attention when researching popular worship music in a city.

As ethnodoxologists and as cocreators, we need to be careful not to overstep our bounds by insisting on authentic (in other words, traditional) music forms. We run the risk, particularly in the power differential between the missionary and the artists typically slanted in favor of the missionary, of pushing our anthropological agendas on other musicians.

Secondly, Schrag advises arts advocates to explore how a Christian community relates artistically to its broader church and cultural context. He suggests applying a "heart arts questionnaire" to the church community including the following question, "If your worship community is multicultural, how could you celebrate diversity in unity? How could

---

7. Schrag and Krabill, *Creating Local Arts Together*, xxiii.
8. Ibid., xxii–xxiii.

each ethnic group feel equally involved, at the same time as drawing people together?"⁹

These are great and important questions, but he has neglected a significant component, that is, generational differences. Division between the generations, most evident in music style proclivities, is a critical element in understanding how a Christian community relates artistically to its broader church and cultural context. Yet it is not even mentioned or acknowledged. Ethnodoxologists need to also ask, "How could each generation feel equally involved, at the same time as drawing people together?" Attention to this vital factor may, in fact, begin to end the worship wars that plague churches across the globe.

Finally, I appreciate Schrag's recognition that relationships are essential. "Our first priority is whole human beings, not just their art forms.... Most of the time it will be your authentic, reciprocal relationship with people that will allow you to enter their lives."[10] There is just no substitute for the currency that relationships bring to research.

My study clearly demonstrates that the most significant impact occurred in the churches with which I had the strongest relationships. Relationships are intentionally built over time. Short-term efforts shortchange impact. There is no shortcut to generating trust. Ethnodoxologists have to clearly recognize what they can and cannot do in a community within a given period of time. To believe you can accomplish more without authentic long-term relationships is a fallacy.

FINAL WORDS

> I'm an artist and a Christian. What is my responsibility? To be a light, to show people what God's done in my life through my music, to shine the values, the transformation, the liberty from sin, and to show God's love to my neighbors.[11]

This research has come full circle. Worship leaders, like Ibraimo, are empowered and passionate about mobilizing music in mission. In this study I have explored the impact of indigenous hymnody and contextual worship arts on the development of church ministry and missions in twelve church contexts in Beira. I discovered the burdens of a noncontextualized

9. Ibid., 177.
10. Ibid., xxxi.
11. Meyers, Ibraimo, worship leader at VFC, field notes, 2014–15.

mission history in music, the challenges of a social hierarchy that robs worship leaders of authority, the practice of a fragmented worship event, and the paucity of theological training through the use of the popular music style *nossa música*.

These discoveries led to the creation of an expanded songwriting workshop model, a multipronged experimental approach to adaptive change through worship praxis. The change process was initiated by critically reflexive focus group interviews at each church. Monthly composer's clubs, rather than a one-time workshop, were conducted over the course of six months. Additional training events and holding environments boosted capacity for enhancing culturally appropriate worship in the local church.

Research data shows that there is now an increased use of local hymnody and a greater mission momentum through music. Pastors are engaged and worship leaders are empowered. Believing musicians are cooperating across denominational lines, worshipping together, and sharing their faith in song. Finally, churches are beginning to intentionally use music to teach, designing cohesive worship-events that communicate clearly and foster spiritual formation.

Contextualized worship arts are an unmistakably critical component of the development of a local church and its members, encouraging personal discipleship, growing ministry, and empowering for mission. Goats in Beira can graze and grow in local pastures, then go further afield, sharing the gospel in song.

APPENDIX A

Research Schedule

Research Phase	Time-Frame	Methods Used	Data Collected
I. General Context (primary case, VFC)	Sept 2012– Apr 2013	Participant Observation	Field notes from: –11 church services –2 music events –8 rehearsals/mtngs
			Videos from: 2 church services
		Interviews	9 semi-structured interviews with pastors, 1 focus group (pilot test)
		Literature Review	Documentation from 46 sources (23 on Mozambique, 23 on Africa)

Appendix A: Research Schedule

Research Phase	Time-Frame	Methods Used	Data Collected
II. Specific Context (cross-case, 12 churches)	Sept 2013–Dec 2013	Participant Observation	Field notes from: - 6 church services - 9 site visits - 4 music events - 20 rehearsals/mtngs - 2 composer's clubs (pilot tests) - 7 IBS classes Videos from: - 9 site visits - 4 music events - 2 composer's clubs - 7 IBS classes
		Interviews	10 structured interviews with pastors
		Summative Content Analysis	154 songs (9 churches)
III. Adaptive Change Experiments (applied research)	Jan 2014–Aug 2014	Participant Observation	Field notes from: - 13 church services - 11 site visits - 3 music events - 11 rehearsals/mtngs - 3 composer's clubs - 12 jam sessions - 3 worship leader's small groups - 12 voice classes - 7 informal conversations Videos from: - 11 site visits - 3 music events - 3 composer's clubs - 3 jam sessions - 1 worship leader's small group

Appendix A: Research Schedule 135

Research Phase	Time-Frame	Methods Used	Data Collected
		Interviews (Focus Groups)	9 focus groups in 9 churches
		Experimental Interventions	Holding Environments: - 12 vocal technique classes - 12 jam sessions - 3 worship leader's small groups
			3 Composer's Clubs
IV. Change Evaluation	Sept 2014– Oct 2014	Participant Observation	Field notes from 5 church services, 2 music events, 4 rehearsals/mtngs, 1 composer's club
		Interviews	10 worship leaders, 6 pastors, 3 research partners
		Questionnaire	40 respondents

APPENDIX B

Case Summaries

FAMÍLIA VITORIOSA (Victory Family Center)

Figure 15: Pastor João Salvador Sitoe

Família Vitoriosa (VFC) was founded by a mixed group of missionaries, (two Brazilian, three Singaporean) in 1998. The church began by meeting in small groups in various areas of the city, and on December 13, 1998, had the first collective worship in the same place where it still meets today. At the time, the church was called Calvary Charismatic Center, better known as CCC.

By 2000, having grown to about 200 adults and 100–150 children, the church started reproducing, planting five other churches in the following three years in Inhamizua, Manica, Buzi, Gorongosa, and Maputo. The same year, VFC started a worship movement called Noite Gospel

(Gospel Night), sponsored by the church band called Ministério International de Louvor Livre Adoração (International Ministry of Praise Free Worship). At that time, VFC was the only church in Beira that used all basic (western) musical instruments. The only other churches that used Western musical instruments just had keyboards. Two years later, VFC started a school of music, praise, and worship called Escola Para Adoradores (School for Worshippers). Many of the great worship bands today, at least in Beira, are a result of that school. VFC continues to be an authority in the area of praise and worship in the evangelical church community of Beira.

VFC still retains a passion for missions in Mozambique. Its vision statement, "Our mission is missions" is evident in the words boldly painted above the church door, "*Sai Missionário*" (Leave a Missionary). One cannot miss the charge as one exits the building. Many young people have shown a great desire to pursue missions and church planting. One young missionary was recently sent to the neighboring province of Manica and is now pastoring a church of twenty-two people, and two additional churches have now been planted around the city of Beira.

The church today is comprised mostly of young people, many who are still in school (either high school or university). There are a few working professionals, and only two elderly members. VFC values discipleship. From the day a person enters the church, they are contacted and challenged to attend the Bible courses and to join a small group. Leaders of small groups are primarily responsible for discipling new believers. This means that almost 80 percent of the church is receiving education and spiritual training for the work of ministry.

VISÃO NA PALAVRA DE DEUS (Vision in the Word of God)

Figure 16: Pastor Jeito Mandongue José (and wife, Marta)

Visão na Palavra de Deus (VPD) is a church with a long and complicated history. The original group of churches were planted as Zionist churches in Sofala Province starting in 1945 when Pedro Sola Chigogoro returned from South Africa where he had become a Christian in a Zionist church. During the late 1960s, non-Catholics experienced tremendous persecution by the Portuguese and Pedro Sola was imprisoned. After his release, the Zionist church sent him to Maputo (the capital) to find a church that would provide protection from the Portuguese. The church he found was Fé dos Apóstolos (Faith of the Apostles Church) (FDA).

FDA was founded by an *assimilado* (assimilated) Mozambican who worked in the post office. He had become a Christian in Swaziland in a Faith Apostolic Mission church. In 1948, FDA was recognized as a church by the Portuguese government. As an AIC with dancing, traditional drums, and green robes for the pastors, it was closer to the Zionist churches, which used white robes. However, the Zionists had to agree to start wearing shoes in church and give up their double-headed drums (and associated dancing style).

A few years after independence in 1975, FRELIMO (the national independence party) arrested Pastor Pedro Sola and put him in jail in Chimoio, because he was in a church with links to the former Portuguese government.

Divisions developed in the FDA church. There were those who were, essentially, Zionist (practicing divination under the auspices of "prophesy," polygamy, and services for the dead), operating under the law of Moses, "*sem sapatos*" (without shoes). Others followed a more typical Pentecostal, evangelical approach, "*com sapatos*" (with shoes). Various other Zionist groups had also joined FDA to escape persecution under the Portuguese. Apparently, they had ignored the requirement to drop certain Zionist practices. This division continued from the late 1980s until 2012, when finally, after repeated attempts to reconcile and unite, Pastor Jeito and others in his branch of FDA realized they'd be discredited if they continued to minister under the FDA label.

They are now operating under a new name, VPD, with a renewed emphasis on evangelism. VPD continues to struggle with its past history, and Pastor Jeito's main concern continues to be syncretism and church discipline. However, there is a growing group of believers who have been trained at IBS and whose theological preparation is strengthening the body.

ASSEMBLEIA DE DEUS INTERNACIONAL
(Assembly of God International)

Figure 17: Pastor Agustinho José Xavier (Lázaro)

Pastor Lázaro is probably one of the oldest and most respected pastors in Beira (eighty-three and counting). His conversion story as a young man is an incredible story of miraculous healing and spiritual warfare through the persistence of a man from a Zionist church. Lázaro was baptized in the church, and within three years began preaching and evangelizing.

He joined the military for twelve or so years, using his salary to support ongoing ministry. During that time he connected with an Assemblies of God missionary in Manga and began to realize that the Zionists were unbiblical. This lead to a confrontation with the Zionist leaders, but resulted in being released to "continue your work for God."

Lázaro did just that, starting a church out of his home, then using an ECD church building. Jealousy due to the rapid growth forced them to move into the only available space, the cemetery. The church was officially registered with the government as Assembléia de Deus Internaçional.

Pastor Lázaro's military connections with PIDE (Portuguese police) led to his eventual imprisonment and torture, and yet, though his cell mates told him he would die, he had a dream of an angel visitation, and was released that evening. He didn't realize he was released until he arrived at his house, full of believers from the church praying for his release.

Lázaro was bi-vocational (continuing his military career while also spearheading a denomination) for many years until it finally became too difficult to balance the demands of both. He decided to leave the military for ministry. When asked, "Why do you want to leave?" he replied, "To do the work of the Lord." His boss as well as his wife thought he was crazy. Yet, through this time of trusting he stated, "This is where I learned about God as a provider."

Today the denomination has churches in every province, stretching from Rovuma to Maputo, and from Beira to Zimbabwe, and is currently starting a church in neighboring Malawi. ADI has approximately five-thousand workers, and about five-hundred churches, fourteen in and around Beira alone. It is truly a Mozambican church, self-supporting, self-governing, and self-sustaining.

UNIÃO BATISTA (Baptist Union)

Figure 18: Pastor Manuel Pequenino (on right) with coworkers

União Batista (UB) is a WIC, started by AEF (now a part of SIM) and a Swedish mission. Its sister church is the United Baptist Church of Zimbabwe, also started by AEF.

It has churches in all ten provinces, and is headquartered in Maputo. In Beira there are now four UB churches.

Appendix B: Case Summaries   141

Figure 19: Youth President Teófilo

Teófilo has been working with youth for over ten years and is now the president of the youth delegation. He shared with me that many people believe that it is the youth's job to come and sing in the church. When he became part of the leadership he wanted to change this mentality. "Youth can do more than just sing," he said. His hope is that youth continue to receive training in leadership, and begin to take on greater responsibilities in the church.

Modernism and the influence of technology is affecting believers, people are more worried about the things of the world than the reign of God. Teófilo believes that the church is not prepared. He said, "I'm not conservative, but we need to monitor this better, especially with the youth who are the future of the church. What type of leaders will we have?"

NOVA ALIANÇA (New Covenant)

Figure 20: Pastor Luis Jofessa Nyazeze

Pastor Nyazeze is another "older generation" pastor who has faithfully worked for decades with SIL to complete a Bible translation in Sena. His dream at seventy-three is to see the translation to completion, to finish seminary (he's in his final year at IBS), and to start helping train pastors out in the rural districts who have few resources and scant biblical training.

After hearing about this research in worship, he shared that this area was also a big interest of his. "People want to worship, not just God, but other ancestors and spirits." He explained that music in the village (i.e., songs sung to call spirits at a healing ceremony) also makes people "fall" like people who are "slain in the spirit" in church.

Mozambique's Catholic mission history was especially vulnerable to syncretism. Nyazeze bluntly stated, "It's worth it to become a Christian because it's easier, you get help and you feel loved, but you don't want to leave everything behind. The real question is, who are we worshipping, and why?"

Nyazeze is the provincial superintendent of the Nova Aliança (NA) denomination, planted by "First Mission" from South Africa decades ago. It is "mini-pentecostal" in that people speak in tongues and have a conservative biblical doctrine. Early input from Plymouth Brethren also resulted in the practice of weekly communion and head coverings for women.

Pastor Nyazeze lamented that an estimated 50–60 percent of Sena speakers started at Nova Aliança but then moved on to start other churches. "I don't know if this is a bad spirit, or God's blessing," he confessed, "but it's probably because our founders were divisive and the younger generation saw and believed that this was an acceptable action." He hopes one day to reunite the two churches (both called Nova Aliança), and to forge an integrated future.

EVANGELHO COMPLETO DE DEUS
(Full Gospel Church of God)

Figure 21: Pastor Mafucha Madoda Mateus

Evangelho Completo de Deus (ECD) has a long history. The denomination, known as Full Gospel Church of God in Africa and Church of God World Mission in the US, started when some American Baptists began speaking in tongues and were removed from the denomination. After praying and fasting, a new church was born. A youth delegation came to South Africa as part of an evangelical church planting mission, and brought the denomination to the continent of Africa.

Miners from Mozambique were exposed to this church while working in South Africa and they brought the denomination back to Mozambique in 1928, officially registered with the government in 1939. It has now spread to all the provinces in Mozambique (except Niassa), and has also moved on to Angola.

Pastor Madoda, though he runs a copy shop near the main market in Beira, is the superintendent of the Sofala Province, in charge of eight districts. Beira alone now has sixteen parishes. They all meet together for worship on the second Sunday of each month.

Madoda confided that ECD has a complicated history, spiritually strong, with lots of faith, but is lagging behind in terms of teaching and resources. "I can't hide," he said. "Quantity we have, quality we don't." He expressed concerns about syncretism, sharing that even the pastors will go to the curandeiros (witch doctors) when they're sick.

ASSEMBLEIA DE DEUS EVANGÊLICA
(Evangelical Assembly of God)

Figure 22: Pastor Alexandre João Maunze

Assembleia de Deus Evangêlica (ADE) started through the efforts of a Canadian missionary working in South Africa with Mozambican miners from Gaza. Upon the miners' return to Mozambique, they preserved the link until the mission came to visit and established a church. From Gaza it spread south to Maputo and was linked with the Swiss Church. From Maputo it spread north to Beira where they initially met in a Methodist church building.

Meanwhile, a Mozambican domestic worker in Zimbabwe named Ofrisse entered a church and the preacher told him to return to Mozambique. Though he couldn't read, he was offered a Bible by a drunkard who said, "I'm giving you life." Upon returning home, praying with the Bible open on his lap, a darkness overtook him, then a light came in front of him, dispersing the darkness. He looked down at the Bible and found that he miraculously could read the words on the pages. He immediately began preaching, returning to Gorongoza and establishing churches there that linked up with the newly established ADE churches in Beira. Currently there are churches established in seven of Mozambique's ten provinces.

Pastor Alexandre's church is known for focusing on the power of the Holy Spirit and the word of God. He blithely stated, "We talk about sin here, people who don't want to hear about sin normally don't stop here!" He went on to remark, "The only way you get prosperity here is from obedience to God. Prosperity comes after obedience."

PRIMEIRA IGREJA BAPTISTA (First Baptist Church)

Figure 23: Pastors Manuel Moises Quembo and Arão Simone Mbulu

During colonial times the Catholic church was "married" to the Portuguese state in Mozambique. This meant that, although Pastor Arão's parents were with the free Methodist church and Arão had been baptized as an infant, the state law required Arão to also be baptized in the Catholic church before he could pass the third grade. Later, he chuckled, he was also baptized Baptist.

Prior to the war for independence the Methodist and Baptist churches only worked with white residents (resulting in a small congregation of about twenty). However, once the war started, they opened the door to black Mozambicans and by 1978 they didn't have a pastor, as all the whites had left.

The following year, Pastor Arão took over the leadership of the Baptist church, which was in Maputo, Gaza, Dondo, and Beira. At that time, the focus was to train national workers in order to evangelize the country with a goal to reach all ten provinces by the 1980s. This goal has finally been reached.

Evangelical churches really grew during the civil war. Arão stated, "The whole world was desperate, they wanted to come to the church for hope, medicine, food, clothes. The church was the only refuge."

I asked about the various Baptist denominations around town (from Baptista Independente, to Baptista Renovada, to the first and second Baptist churches). Arão explained that the second Baptist church is the daughter of the first Baptist church, but that the others split off from the convention for various reasons (disciplinary action, or doctrinal differences). Currently there are approximately 130 churches in the Baptist Convention in Mozambique.

Pastor Arão is now retired, having just turned seventy-two, but is still quite active in evangelism and missions. Pastor Quembo now leads the flock at the first Baptist church. His hope is that each believer grows in their knowledge of God and lives what they're learning. "We need work in contextualization," Quembo stated. "What we've received is a hymnal. The Baptist missionaries didn't really connect with our African music culture that is alive, that we dance to. People need to be encouraged to worship God as they are."

MISSÃO EVANGÊLICA DA VIDA NOVA
(Evangelical Mission of New Life)

Figure 24: Pastor Tomás Pereira Viageiro

Missão Evangêlica da Vida Nova (MEVN) is a relatively young independent church, planted eight years ago in loose affiliation with the Assemblies of God denomination. It has already spread to Pemba and Chimoio and has plans to go to Maputo and Lichinga.

Their mission vision is to reach people between fifteen and forty-five years of age, with the principle goal of reaching youth in universities. Pastor Tomás works to show his congregation a balance between theology and science. "Many people get to university and then leave the church because they are confronted with new worldviews (i.e., evolution)," he said. "We want to be culturally, spiritually, and intellectually relevant in society."

MEVN has a young, educated, cosmopolitan congregation. They dress casually (Americans should read "casual" in this case as "business smart"), use PowerPoint, and have recently moved from renting a conference room in a high-rise building in the middle of downtown Beira to their newly constructed church building. The teaching is simple and direct and the biblical doctrine is basic.

MEVN is known for networking and connecting with others for further training. "We don't have a monopoly of knowledge about Jesus. One can't receive everything one needs from one pastor, so we ask God to help us be alert to others who can help us."

Pastor Tomás' main concern is leadership training, building capacity in his leaders. This takes time, resources, and patience. He constantly works toward leadership formation, asking, "Have they captured the vision?"

AURORA MESSIÂNICA (Messianic Dawn)

Figure 25: Pastor Feliciano Adriano Cohauela

Pastor Adriano was born into a Christian family, but his parents attended a church that wasn't Pentecostal. He attended IBS, then another Bible school for additional training. In the third year, during the church-planting phase, there were internal conflicts that eventually led to him striking out on his own, planting Aurora Messiânica in 2004.

Aurora Messiânica has three cell churches in Beira and one new church plant in Zambézia (with twenty members), 350 members in all. They have a large piece of land in Zambézia (where Adriano was born) and plans are in the works to construct a training center from which to launch further mission efforts into Northern Mozambique (which is predominantly Muslim).

One of the unique characteristics of Aurora Messiânica is that the majority of its members were drawn to the church due to its practical ministry to the neighborhood by providing the only school within walking distance. This school, started shortly after the church was planted, now has over 1,000 students, and is registered as a state school, though they provide Christian education. Even though Aurora Messiânica is literally next-door to a mosque, people are drawn to a church that meets their practical needs for education.

Training in worship is one of Pastor Adriano's primary concerns. "If we get leaders trained for worship, this will have positive results on the church as a whole. We need spiritual fire!"

ASSEMBLEIA DE DEUS AFRICANO
(African Assemblies of God)

Figure 26: Pastor Anacleto Luis Ferrão (deceased)

Appendix B: Case Summaries 149

Ezekiel Mbiti, a Zimbabwean, founded the denomination Assembleia de Deus Africano (ADA) on May 12, 1960. In 1969 it moved from Zimbabwe to Mozambique via Pastor Simão, spreading east to Beira and then moving both north and south. During the war for independence, the newly formed government inadvertently helped the promulgation of the denomination, through the humiliation of imprisonment and persecution.

Today ADA (also known as Forward in Faith Ministry International) sends out missionaries from Mozambique to Brazil, Portugal, and other Lusophone (Portuguese-speaking) nations. These missionaries (estimated fifteen to twenty) are sustained by local tithes and offerings.

ADA is known for being a strong, financially independent church that speaks a lot about money. This is directly linked to the founder's philosophy of financial sustainability and lack of a formal education. When offered financial support from the US, he declined, preferring to have a church sustained through internal means. These two factors have contributed to a closed mentality to outsiders, which continues today.

Pastor Anacleto (self-admittedly a bit of a rebel and a trend-setter) was the district supervisor of ADA for a number of years. However, as he refused to transfer to Chimoio due to health concerns, he stepped back from a supervisory role. He pastored two small local ADA churches until his death.

He believed that worship is powerful. In one local congregation he challenged them to start a prayer and worship service even without a building, promising, "We'll see good things when we worship God!" Sure enough, the following day, a Korean approached the group and offered to pay for all the construction costs. The church was, quite literally, built on praise!

AMERICAN BOARD (United Church of Christ)

Figure 27: Pastor José Francisco Madeira

American Congregationalist missionaries, through the American Board of Commissioners for Foreign Missions, first arrived in Beira on July 19, 1892, ironically the same day that the Mozambique Company became the charter administrator of Beira, and the territories of Sofala and Manica. Unfortunately, their efforts in Beira were stymied substantially, particularly by Portuguese concern about "foreign" encroachment on company territory. They finally abandoned Beira in 1917.

However, in 1932, an opportunity for constructive American support of an indigenous church in Beira surfaced in the person of Pierre Loze and Tapera Nkomo. By March 1933, Loze was holding regular meetings in his house with groups of 120–150 people in attendance. Though early years were marked by hostility and conflict between two Protestant religious associations, there was also evidence of growth. Freire, a Portuguese evangelical, drafted a hymn during a 1938 visit:

> Association, spread your light
> Many heathen have yet to be saved;
> Manica, Sofala do not know Jesus
> Let us go, full of love, to call them.

In some ways, the isolation from the outside world and the fractionism within perhaps created a stronger and more contextualized Protestant ministry. However, the associations faced a greater challenge when the first Bishop of Beira arrived in Sofala in 1944 and dissolved both associations.

Freire objected and finally managed to gain permission to conduct an evangelical ministry effort through a new organization, Igreja Evangélica Portuguesa Africana de Moçambique (Evangelical Church of Portuguese Africa in Mozambique). In this way, the work continued, isolated from outside support, but primarily in the hands of Mozambican leadership.

APPENDIX C

Sample Event Observation Report

FN CULTO @ Vila Massane "*Igreja Mãe*" da ADI (10/13/13)

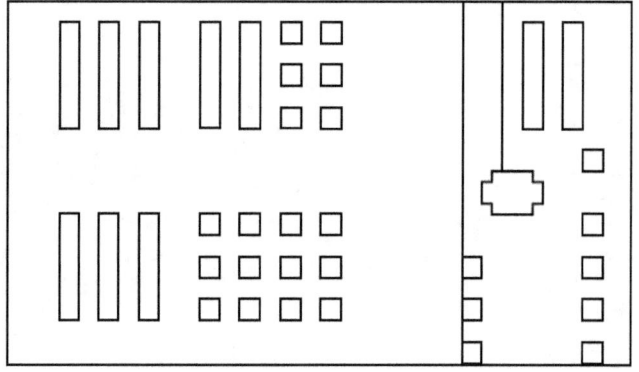

Figure 28: Map of Vila Massane (ADI)

ARTIFACTS

8 posters "*Querido Irmão manter o telephone no silêncio ao entrar na igreja*"

Plastic chairs, wooden chairs, benches

Plants

Pulpit

Batuque (one outside heating up, one in front of pulpit)

Fans

Clock (not working)

Curtains

Raised front platform and rail in front of seating area

Construction material (wood, iron, wheelbarrow)

Bell, used to quiet people down during prayers or singing

ACTORS

P. Vitor

P. Mesa (showed up at end)

Jose Melo (choir master)

Valentim

Taddeu (met us at the church)

Youth choir (Industria and VM)

Secretary/translator

MC

ACTIVITIES

Though I'd agreed to meet Taddeu at my house (as I didn't know where the church was) he called me that morning and told me he was already on the road and would meet me at Paragem das Niveis. As I didn't know where that was exactly, and Brian couldn't give me good enough directions, I begged Valentim to go with me. It ended up being a really good idea as he knows the road to Manga well, he enjoyed the service, and he filled in where Taddeu didn't man up.

Valentim and I met Taddeu at the chapa stop and arrived at the church around 9:15. One elder man was sweeping the church. We got set up and I realized I'd left my camera card behind. I tried using the video camera but the mini SD card wasn't formatted. Sigh. Also had problems with my pens. Technology!

People slowly started trickling in, sitting quietly, pausing to pray, reading Bible, texting, kids quietly chattering, youth brings in batuki that's been warming up in the sun.

At 9:47 a man turns on the fans (thankfully) and asks youth to start as the time is running out. The few youth that are already seated stand up and call the congregation to pray. We all stand and pray loudly together. Various youth lead out in song after song, we pray again ("*Vamos ir a presença de Deus*") and after a final song we sit.

In the midst of this initial song time, Pastor Vitor (whom I've yet to meet) pulls me aside outside and introduces himself. He apologized that half of the youth choir was at another church conference in Manga. He said that they were expecting me last week. I profusely apologized, explaining how I couldn't make it due to Brian being at a conference and that I'd called P. Mesa and P. Lazaro to explain my absence. I don't know if he'd gotten the message or not. Then he asked if I was going to help him preach.

I responded that while I was honored for the invitation, my primary responsibility at the service was to observe and take notes, but that I'd be willing to greet the church. He agreed and we went back in to service.

The MC gives a call to worship: We live in the grace of God and so we worship Him.

- We've left the worship time and now we'd like to welcome the pastor and Megan.

Testimonies (asking for two men, two women, and youth) . . . we pass our faith and strength on to others (youth choir left to prepare). . . . Simple refrain was sung as "filler" until someone got up to testify.

1. Young woman: Six months ago I was in Maputo, He protects me and guards me
2. Young man: I was "*incomodado*" (ill) but I prayed to God and I felt His presence and I was healed.
3. Man: My father died, I'm alone, I'm returning to Inhambane so I'm saying goodbye.

I was invited to greet the church. I stood up and said a little something (I think I need to prepare this better, I'm going to have to do this at each church and I really flopped it, forgetting to even introduce myself!)

Machaze, greeted the church. . . . He's going to be regularly attending as he's moved out to Manga.

Secretary: Announcements:

- thanks to God today is the day to collect *dizimos* (tithes)
- we'll be worshipping in another church
- anniversary shirts and CDs still available
- someone died, funeral already happened, last day to pray, we'll go as a church after service
- need one pianist, two singers, and two prayers for the "*Nova Geração*" youth church, crusade 24–27th

    (space-filler music)

INDUSTRIA CHOIR: choir director snaps fingers in and out to direct and quietly sings first line to give pitches

- as they sing people clap and one youth yells out, "*Faia*" (fire, as in "that's hot!")

VM CHOIR: entrance shuffle song

- soloists stand in front corner

MC, service has four parts, we're now moving into the third part. The first is the time when you arrive early and pray/praise/worship. The second part is the preaching part, where you receive the word of God. The third part is the altar offering (songs are sung and youth pass wooden boxes through the congregation).

Megan, bless the offering. I asked them all to stand and I prayed.

SS went away to class, three more announcements.

MC, we'll sing one more strong and alive song to call God's presence before the sermon. The pastor has to preach and pray. Let's sing so that the pastor only has to preach.

* song

Sermon, *Reino dos Ceus* (P. Vitor flipped back and forth between Portuguese and Ndau, the poor translator had to really work to keep up not just with the language flips but also with pastor's animated preaching style).

Luke 17:20–21 (get your notebooks and pens)

> The reign of God is in us—justice, peace, joy in the HS
>
>> Rom 14:17; Rom 3:22; 1 Cor 2:15; Neh 8:10

You are the church . . . the reign of God is in YOU!

Regular call and response. . . . Amen? Amen. Hallelujah? Amen!

P. Vitor turned and asked me, "Is being *'avarento'* a sin?" It took me awhile to realize he was asking me a question, then it took me awhile to understand what the question was, then I didn't know what *avarento* meant. Thankfully, someone finally said that *avarento* means someone who doesn't like to share (avarice). At that point I made a negative face and shook my finger to indicate that I disapproved.

Pastor mercifully moved on from me and said, "Yes, it's a sin, like prostitution."

If the reign of God is in you and it is a sin to be stingy then we need to share the justice, peace, and joy of the HS with others.

> * song, "*Obrigado Jesus*" (different version than I know in Ndau, Port, Eng, back to Ndau)

PRAYER

Invite woman forward to accept Christ, while choir is singing, other leader comes and leads her through a prayer, asking her to face the pulpit with hands raised, then kneeling while he put his hand on her head and prayed. She finally stood and the choir stopped singing.

P. Vitor introduced the woman to the church and said she'd accepted Jesus.

Visitor from Zambezi, greets the church.

> * Welcome song, "*A nossa igreja ama voce*"

Quelimane visitor (wife of Xindi evangelist) greeted the church:

- passed offering plates for mercy offering for man who was leaving for Inhambane to help pay for funeral expenses

Pastor reprimanded the church (two people had come up and made change in the offering box). He said that the people needed to make change outside the church, not during offering.

Then it was time for tithes. The secretary called up each cell (twenty-three total, but only seventeen showed). The choir would sing, a representative would bring an envelope with the tithes in it and a piece of paper. The secretary would collect, count it up, then ring the bell. The choir would sit down and the secretary would read the total and the names of the people who gave and the amounts.

SS kids appeared at some point in the middle of this last portion of the service.

P. Mesa, I was late due to a funeral, talked a bit about my work and why I was at the service. He also told the church he was leaving for a trip and thanked the youth for their enthusiastic (though somewhat unruly) praise.

I stayed around to briefly talk with P. Mesa and Vitor and to meet the choir leader (Jose Melo). They all asked me to return again, and P. Mesa asked me to consider attending another ADI church. I said I'd like to, but I'll have to see how the time works out. I commended P. Vitor on his preaching and said I really enjoyed the service. He asked why. I said, "It's because people really worshipped God today, and that's the main point, isn't it?"

I asked them all for a collection of songs, and likely will need to follow up with Jose.

APPENDIX D

Field Notes Quoted

Page	Data Type	Source	Location	Date
	Informal interview	Musicians	Megan's car	2009–2010
	Field notes	(Megan)	Church site visit	2013–2014
	Informal interview	Friend	Megan's house	2012–2013
	Focus group	Participant	Church site visit	2013–2014
	Field notes	(Megan)	Church site visit	2013–2014
	Informal interview	Pastor	Coffee shop	2012–2013
	Field notes	(Megan)	Church site visit	2013–2014
	Informal interview	Pastor	Church site visit	2013–2014
	Field notes	MC	Church site visit	2012–2013
	Field notes	MC	Church site visit	2013–2014
	Informal interview	Pastors/musicians	variable	2012–2013
	Focus group	Participant	Church site visit	2013–2014
	Interview	Pastor	Coffee shop	2013–2014
	Field notes	Pastor	Church rehearsal	2012–2013
	Interview	Research assistant	Seminary	2013–2014
	Field notes	Musician	Church rehearsal	2013–2014
	Informal interview	Pastor/musician	Pastor's office	2012–2013

Appendix D: Field Notes Quoted

Page	Data Type	Source	Location	Date
	Field notes	MC	Church site visit	2013–2014
	Interview	Musician	Megan's house	2014–2015
	Focus group	Participant	Small group	2013–2014
	Interview	Pastor	Pastor's office	2012–2013
	Field notes	MC	Church site visit	2012–2013
	Field notes	MC	Church site visit	2013–2014
	Field notes	MC	Church site visit	2013–2014
	Informal interview	Research assistant	Coffee shop	2013–2014
	Informal interview	Research assistant	Megan's house	2013–2014
	Interview	Pastor	Pastor's office	2013–2014
	Focus group	(Megan)	Composer's club	2013–2014
	Focus group	Participant	Composer's club	2013–2014
	Focus group	Participant	Composer's club	2013–2014
	Focus group	Participants	Composer's club	2013–2014
	Field notes	(Megan)	Church concert	2014–2015
	Interview	Research assistant	Megan's house	2014–2015
	Interview	Research assistant	Megan's house	2014–2015
	Focus group	Participant	Composer's club	2014–2015
	Interview	Research assistant	Megan's house	2014–2015
	Interview	Pastor	Megan's house	2014–2015
	Interview	Pastor	Megan's house	2014–2015
	Interview	Pastor	Pastor's office	2014–2015
	Interview	Pastor	Megan's house	2014–2015
	Interview	Pastor	Pastor's office	2014–2015
	Interview	Pastor	Megan's house	2014–2015
	Interview	Pastor	Pastor's office	2014–2015
	Informal interview	Friend	Megan's house	2012–2013
	Field notes	Musician	Church concert	2014–2015

APPENDIX E

Structured Interview Compiled Responses

THE FOLLOWING INTERVIEW QUESTIONS were taken directly from the Creating Local Arts Together workbook, and modified slightly after pilot testing:[1]

1. What is your church known for doing well?
2. What hopes do you have for children, youth, adults, yourself, the church community?
3. What issues are difficult for your church or cause you significant worry?
4. What church do you admire and why?

Below is a table of compiled responses from ten pastors. Each number corresponds to a question asked.

Pastor:	1	2	3	4
João	Evangelism Helps/service Teaching/ discipleship	Study about family Hope for community	Church registration Leadership	VFC (Singapore) Tabernáculo Aliança da Fé (spiritual fervor)

1. Schrag and Krabill, *Creating Local Arts Together*, 49–51.

Appendix E: Structured Interview Compiled Responses

Pastor:	1	2	3	4
Jeito	Evangelism Teaching	Teaching Hope for community	Syncretism Church discipline	Pastor Bandeira (strong teaching) Peniel (quick growth)
Lázaro	Missions Preaching	Teaching for kids Training future leaders	Training Discipleship	Any church that speaks the Truth
Teófilo	Good Biblical doctrine	Training future leaders	Modernism, influence of technology	1st Baptist (spiritual maturity)
Nhazeze	Mini-Pentecostal conservative Weekly communion	Teaching, training, members stay firm in their faith	Division	Assembleia de Deus (administration)
Madoda	Strong faith, behind in teaching and resources	Big church to confront Muslims Re-initiate praise dept	Syncretism People go to curandeiro	Churches that can sustain their pastors
Alexandre	Preaching obedience	That congregation embraces teaching	Obedience	The church is good, problem is people
Arão & Quembo	Teaching, preaching, evangelism, missions	Believers live what they're learning	Few people have a real thirst for learning the Word	1st Baptist (history) Catholic church (work in ed/society)
Tomás	Networking, events for churches, relevant, casual, welcoming	Leaders well-trained to be salt and light in world	Leadership training, building capacity	VFC (culture of worship)
Adriano	Warm (worship issue), help community	Get leaders trained for worship	Improve church building Trained leaders	Peniel (explosive growth, spiritual fire) Aurora Messianica (impact in community)

Appendix E: Structured Interview Compiled Responses

As indicated, there is considerable consensus even among diverse pastors, training levels, congregations, and denominational affiliations. Though 90 percent of the pastors indicated that they believe their churches to be known for some type of teaching, ironically, 90 percent also admitted that their greatest concern and hope for their church was some type of further leadership training or discipleship. Even the qualities most admired in other churches were spiritual maturity and strong teaching, beating other notable qualities such as worship, church growth, administration, and community impact.

ADMIRED CHURCH QUALITIES

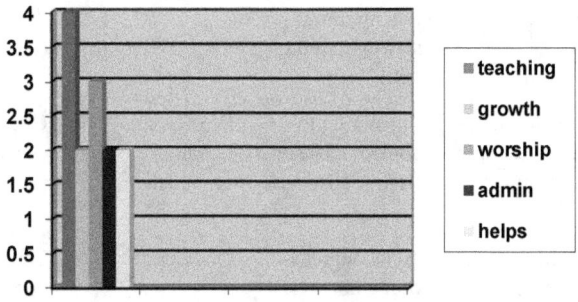

Figure 29: Admired Church Qualities

These pastors' responses confirm my personal ministry experiences and reflections, and casual conversations with church leaders and congregants, that the Mozambican church is a "mile wide, and an inch deep." Sadly, in the last four months I've heard of five young worship leaders who have had to step away from ministry due to immoral choices (pregnancy out of wedlock, fornication, divorce). The need for training strong worship leadership and ministry accountability through ongoing discipleship is clear.

APPENDIX F

Lyric Theology

Subject: God (Theology)

Theme	Song Type	Frequency
God's goodness and greatness	NM/PS	8/5
Rock and salvation	PS	4
Praiseworthy name/praised/exalted	NM/PS	7/3
Deserves our praise/offering	NM/PS	2/3
Father send us	NM	3
Sufficient grace	PS	2
Sustaining presence	PS	3
Tolerant and patient, forgiving	PS/WH	1/1
Alpha and omega	PS	1
Sanctifies/saves/cures	PS	2
Faithful	PS	3
Authority/reigns	NM/PS/WH	1/8/1
Powerful/saves from enemies/protects	NM/PS	9/10
Merciful	PS	1
Hope of Israel/Messiah	NM/PS	1/1
Ebenezer, this far he's helped us	NM	1

Appendix F: Lyric Theology

Theme	Song Type	Frequency
Good plans for believers, keeps promises	PS	1
Eternal	NM/WH	2/3
Just	NM	1
Peace	NM/WH	1/1
Holy Father	NM/WH	1/2
TOTAL: 21		92

NM, 12/21 = 57%; PS, 15/21 = 71%; WH, 5/21 = 24%

Subject: Jesus (Christology)

Theme	Song Type	Frequency
Name praised	NM/WH	1/1
Blood (of Lamb) poured out	NM/PS	3/1
Son of God	NM	1
Died for us, Savior	NM/PS/WH	5/3/5
Exalted (in Spirit)	NM	2
Truth	NM	2
Beloved, love, loves us	NM/PS	3/3
Master	WH	1
Friend	WH	1
Will return	NM	3
Lives	NM/PS	1/1
Unequalled	NM/PS	7/3
Is calling us	NM/WH	2/1
Dominion and power	PS	1
King (of Kings)	PS/WH	2/2
Author and perfector of faith	PS	1
Reason for life	PS	1
Death gives access to Father	PS/WH	2/1
TOTAL: 18		60

NM, 11/18 = 61%; PS, 10/18 = 56%; WH, 7/18 = 39%

Subject: Holy Spirit (pneumatology)

Theme	Song Type	Frequency
One spirit	PS	1
New spirit	PS	2
Unites us	PS	1
Sent by Father	PS	1
Consoles us	PS	1
Brings understanding	WH	1
TOTAL: 6		7

NM, 0/6 = 0%; PS, 5/6 = 83%; WH, 1/6 = 17%

Subject: Believers (anthropology)

Theme	Song Type	Frequency
Building a spiritual church	NM	1
Raised hands (in worship)	NM/PS	1/3
United	NM/PS	2/2
Come to pray	NM	1
Can be saved in Jesus	WH	1
Bow down	NM	1
Sacrifice of praise/thankful	NM/PS	5/2
Have eternal life	NM/PS	2/1
Walk/be with God	NM/PS	6/6
Don't sin, be obedient	NM	1
Similar to Jesus	NM	1
Do the work God gave you	NM	3
Praise and worship	NM/PS	8/7
Need God	NM/PS/WH	1/3/1
Proclaim, preach, announce	NM/PS/WH	2/1/1
Soldiers of Jesus	NM	2

Appendix F: Lyric Theology

Theme	Song Type	Frequency
Valued	PS	1
Temple of Holy Spirit	PS	2
Growing in faith	NM/PS	1/1
Obedient to God's word	NM	2
Don't want to go back/firm	NM/PS	1/1
Transformed life, new heart	PS/WH	1/1
Going to God's house	NM/PS	2/1
Believe in God's son	NM	2
Blessed	NM/WH	1/1
Read Bible and pray to grow	NM	2
Look for Kingdom of God	NM	1
TOTAL: 27		56

NM, 23/27 = 85%; PS, 14/27 = 52%; WH, 5/27 = 19%

Subject: Church (ecclesiology)

Theme	Song Type	Frequency
Body united, family	PS	1

NM, 0/1 = 0%; PS, 1/1 = 100%; WH, 0/1 = 0%

Subject: Afterlife (escatology)

Theme	Song Type	Frequency
Make us cross-over	NM	1
Crown to earn	NM/WH	1/1
World is ending	NM	1
TOTAL: 3		4

NM, 3/3 = 100%; PS, 0/4 = 0%; WH, 1/3 = 33%

CHURCH ACTIVITIES:

Subject: Baptism

Theme	Song Type	Frequency
New life	NM	1
Renewed	PS	1

Subject: Evangelism/Missions

Theme	Song Type	Frequency
Preach/announce good news	NM/WH	5/1
Good news has power	NM	1
Given a field to cultivate	NM	1
Strengthen/follow the good news	NM	3
TOTAL: 4		11

NM, 4/4 = 100%; PS, 0/4 = 0%; WH, 1/4 = 25%

Subject: Offering

Theme	Song Type	Frequency
God deserves offerings	PS	1
We should bring offerings	NM	2
TOTAL: 2		3

Subject: Prayer

Theme	Song Type	Frequency
Power (to defeat Satan)	NM	2
Oil in my heart (passion)	NM	1
Don't stop praying	NM	2
Brings intimacy with God	PS	1
TOTAL: 4		6

APPENDIX G

Questionnaire Data

Questionnaire Results

#	Gender	Church	Clubs	Other	#2	#3
1	M	7DA	2	RJ/Class	Teaching, Practicing	Inspiration to compose
2	F	BR	2	Class	Practicing, Growing	Communicate through music
3	M	BR	3	RJ/Class	Leading on worship team	Helped in my church
4	M	VFC	4		Composing new songs	Capacity to explain to others
5	M	VFC	7	RJ/IL/Class	Composing, Teaching	Confidence in leading
6	F	BR	2	RJ/IL/Class	Leading, Teaching	I'm more confident and open
7	M	ECD	0	Class	Teaching	Helped worship in my church
8	M	ADE	0	Class	Creating a worship team	Need for worship team
9	M	BR	2	RJ/IL/Class	Created a composer's club	Engaged in music in missions
10	M	VPD	1	Class	Leading this in church	Music feeds my faith

Appendix G: Questionnaire Data

#	Gender	Church	Clubs	Other	#2	#3
11	F	VPD	1	Class	Helping my church to grow	Helped in song selection
12	M	VFC	6	RJ	Composing, Practicing	Better understanding of worship
13	F	MCA	0	RJ/IL/Class	Leading, Teaching	Transform lives through music
14	M	1st B	3	RJ/IL/Class	Teaching	Learned how to lead worship
15	F	VFC	1			The importance of music
16	M	VFC	3		Leading on worship team	Understand what worship is
17	M	VCM	2	RJ/Class	Preaching the gospel	Helped personally and in church
18	M	VCM	0	RJ/Class	Preaching through worship	Teaching through music
19	M	ADE	0	RJ	Leading	Improved the quality of worship
20	M	1st B	1	RJ	Evangelism	Acquiring knowledge
21	M	VFC	4–6		Using worship in a better way	Activating our worship
22	F	A M	2		Learning, teaching others	It's helped a lot in my church
23	M	ECD	5	RJ/Class	Learning	Contributed positively
24	M	ADI	5	Class	Leading, Composing	Positively
25	M	ADI	3	IL/Class	Leading revival meetings	Personally and in my church
26	M	G U	1		Teaching	Personally
27	F	VFC	5		Practicing	Implemented in church
28	M	1st B	0	Class	Sharing, seeking more	Significance of music we sing

Appendix G: Questionnaire Data

#	Gender	Church	Clubs	Other	#2	#3
29	M	VPD	1	RJ	Sharing gospel through music	Contributed positively
30	M	VFC	2	RJ	Composing	Defined the purpose and themes
31	F	1st B	0	Class	Practicing, Ministering	Improved a lot
32	M	1st B	0	Class		I learned a lot, it helped
33	M	VPD	0	Class		Yes, in each place
34	M	VFC	2	Class	Practicing	It helped a lot, edified us
35	M	1st B	0	Class	God is interested in worship	The HS helps us worship Him
36	M	2nd B	3	RJ, class	Leading on worship team	For me, it helped a lot
37	M	1st B	0	Class	Practicing	Yes, but we need more
38	F	1st B	0	Class	Practicing	Worshipping God
39	M	VFC	4		Composing	Helped the church a lot
40	M	VFC	3		Leading	Helped personally and in church

Clubs and Other Activities

#	Gender	Church	Clubs	Other	#2	#3
1	M	7DA	2	RJ/Class	Teaching, Practicing	Inspiration to compose
2	F	BR	2	Class	Practicing, Growing	Communicate through music
3	M	BR	3	RJ/Class	Leading on worship team	Helped in my church

Appendix G: Questionnaire Data

#	Gender	Church	Clubs	Other	#2	#3
5	M	VFC	7	RJ/IL/Class	Composing, Teaching	Confidence in leading
6	F	BR	2	RJ/IL/Class	Leading, Teaching	I'm more confident and open
9	M	BR	2	RJ/IL/Class	Created a composer's club	Engaged in music in missions
10	M	VPD	1	Class	Leading this in church	Music feeds my faith
11	F	VPD	1	Class	Helping my church to grow	Helped in song selection
12	M	VFC	6	RJ	Composing, Practicing	Better understanding of worship
14	M	1st B	3	RJ/IL/Class	Teaching	Learned how to lead worship
17	M	VCM	2	RJ/Class	Preaching the gospel	Helped personally and in church
20	M	1st B	1	RJ	Evangelism	Acquiring knowledge
23	M	ECD	5	RJ/Class	Learning	Contributed positively
24	M	ADI	5	Class	Leading, Composing	Positively
25	M	ADI	3	IL/Class	Leading revival meetings	Personally and in my church
29	M	VPD	1	RJ	Sharing gospel through music	Contributed positively
30	M	VFC	2	RJ	Composing	Defined the purpose and themes
34	M	VFC	2	Class	Practicing	It helped a lot, edified us
36	M	2nd B	3	RJ, class	Leading on worship team	For me, it helped a lot

Appendix G: Questionnaire Data

Clubs Alone

#	Gender	Church	Clubs	Other	#2	#3
4	M	VFC	4		Composing new songs	Capacity to explain to others
15	F	VFC	1			The importance of music
16	M	VFC	3		Leading on worship team	Understand what worship is
21	M	VFC	4–6		Using worship in a better way	Activating our worship
22	F	A M	2		Learning, Teaching others	It's helped a lot in my church
26	M	G U	1		Teaching	Personally
27	F	VFC	5		Practicing	Implemented in church
39	M	VFC	4		Composing	Helped the church a lot
40	M	VFC	3		Leading	Helped personally and in church

No Clubs

#	Gender	Church	Clubs	Other	#2	#3
7	M	ECD	0	Class	Teaching	Helped worship in my church
8	M	ADE	0	Class	Creating a worship team	Need for worship team
13	F	MCA	0	RJ/IL/Class	Leading, Teaching	Transform lives through music)
18	M	VCM	0	RJ/Class	Preaching through worship	Teaching through music
19	M	ADE	0	RJ	Leading	Improved the quality of worship
28	M	1st B	0	Class	Sharing, Seeking more	Significance of music we sing

#	Gender	Church	Clubs	Other	#2	#3
31	F	1st B	o	Class	Practicing, Ministering	Improved a lot
32	M	1st B	o	Class		I learned a lot, it helped
33	M	VPD	o	Class		Yes, in each place
35	M	1st B	o	Class	God is interested in worship	The HS helps us worship Him
37	M	1st B	o	Class	Practicing	Yes, but we need more
38	F	1st B	o	Class	Practicing	Worshipping God

APPENDIX H

Follow-Up Structured Interview Compiled Responses

I interviewed six pastors using the following questions:

1. What are you thinking about worship in your church today?
2. Has the work that I've done contributed in some way to the vision God has given you?
3. Could we do better? What's missing?

My goal in these interviews was to ascertain impact inside the local church, whether pastors were indeed drawing on the multiple training opportunities to shape their congregations.

Pastor	Church	1	2	3
João	VFC	Comprehension better, still need practice, we are composing, everyone participates	H changed the night of the focus group interview, church isn't complaining about worship ministry anymore	Can't comment until restoration process is over
Arão	1stB	Need a worship pastor, better organization	Contributed positively, people are asking for more training	Need more time and more training

Appendix H: Follow-Up Structured Interview Compiled Responses

Pastor	Church	1	2	3
Jeito	VPD	Worship group not practicing b/c demoralized (inst. broken)	We know good worship helps, but we're still not practicing these things	Sure, depends on what you can do . . . content needs to be biblical
Nhazeze	NA	Reasonably acceptable, but suspect syncretism, still songs w/out biblical content	Contributed to help me think and reflect on what praise and worship is, helped me personally pay attention to words	Didn't do a focus group, conflict between generations in worship, worship training course at new Bible school
Adriano	AM	Still trying to resolve worship war	We've included worship as topic at general conference	Need to figure out a way to address worship war, need more training
Alexandre	ADE	Worship group is rising to challenge of ministry calling	Clarifications and corrections have been made, growing interest in composing locally	Informed praise is a tremendous power, you've helped us understand the reality of worship!

Vita

Music and mission have always been a part of Megan's life. Megan Marie Meyers was born to Chumley and Connie Eckerle (a music teacher and choir director) on October 19, 1975, in Stayton, Oregon. As a family, they moved to Papua New Guinea in 1983 with Wycliffe Bible Translators. Following graduation from Ukarumpa High School, she began studies in cultural anthropology at Occidental College, in Los Angeles, California, where she received her Bachelor of Arts. She is a pianist and vocal performer, and has taught music lessons throughout her adult life.

Her graduate studies began at Fuller Theological Seminary where she pursued a master's degree in ethnomusicology. She paid her way through school by becoming a children's fine-arts instructor and teaching salsa and swing lessons in a friend's dance studio. While completing a songwriting workshop practicum in Ivory Coast, she met her husband, also a missionary kid. They were married shortly after graduation in 2003, where they became involved in an inner-city church plant and a Christian community development after school arts ministry in Detroit, Michigan.

During a visit to Mozambique in 2005, the Meyers sensed God's gentle nudge to consider ministry there. Three children and a vision trip later, Megan and Brian Meyers were appointed with WorldVenture as missionaries to Beira, Mozambique, in 2009. During these first two years of ministry through ethnomusicology, Megan realized the need for further training and deeper investigation into the music-culture of churches in Beira.

The Meyers returned to Beira in 2012 (now with four children), where Megan continued to teach worship courses at local seminaries, conduct songwriting workshops, offer worship consultations, and train worship leaders and church musicians.

In her spare time, she enjoys painting, planting in the garden, and playing her mbira (thumb piano). Her passion is to inspire the creation of contextualized worship arts as a key component of the development of the local church and its members, encouraging personal discipleship, growing ministry, and empowering for mission.

References Cited

Agawu, V. Kofi. *Representing African Music: Postcolonial Notes, Queries, Positions.* New York: Routledge, 2003.
Avery, Tom. "Music of the Heart: The Power of Indigenous Worship in Reaching Unreached Peoples with the Gospel." *Mission Frontiers* 18 (1996) 13–14.
Barnlund, Dean C. "A Transactional Model of Communication." In *Communication Theory*, edited by C. David Mortensen, 42–57. New Brunswick, NJ: Transaction, 2008.
Barz, Gregory. *Singing for Life: HIV/AIDS and Music in Uganda.* New York: Routledge, 2006.
Bebey, Francis. *African Music: A People's Art.* New York: Lawrence Hill, 1975.
Berliner, Paul. *The Soul of Mbira: Music and Traditions of the Shona People of Zimbabwe.* Berkeley: University of California Press, 1981.
Bernard, H. Russell. *Social Research Methods: Qualitative and Quantitative Approaches.* Thousand Oaks, CA: SAGE, 2000.
Bevans, Stephen B., and Roger P. Schroeder. *Constants in Context: A Theology of Mission for Today.* Maryknoll, NY: Orbis, 2004.
Blacking, John. "Eight Flute Tunes from Butembo East Belgian Congo, an Analysis in Two Parts, Musical and Physical." *African Music* 1 (1955) 24–52.
Bohlman, Philip. *World Music: A Very Short Introduction.* New York: Oxford University Press, 2002.
Bosch, David. "An Emerging Paradigm for Mission." *Missiology* 11 (1983) 485–510.
Bulatao, Jaime C. "Split-Level Christianity." In *Phenomena and Their Interpretation: Landmark Essays, 1957–1989*, by Jaime C. Bulatao, 22–32. Manila: Ateneo de Manila, 1992.
Chamango, Simão. *A Chegada do Evangelho em Moçambique.* 2nd ed. Maputo, Mozambique, 1994.
Chan, Simon. "Mother Church: Toward a Pentecostal Ecclesiology." *Pneuma* 22 (2000) 189.
Chernoff, John Miller. *African Rhythm and African Sensibility.* Chicago: University of Chicago Press, 1979.
Cherry, Constance. *The Worship Architect.* Grand Rapids, MI: Baker, 2010.

References Cited

Chitando, Ezra. *Singing Culture: A Study of Gospel Music in Zimbabwe*. Uppsala, Sweden: Nordiska Afrikainstitutet, 2002.

Central Intelligence Agency (CIA). *World Fact Book*. https://www.cia.gov/library/publications/the-world-factbook/fields/2122.html.

Conn, Harvie. *Eternal Word and Changing Worlds: Theology, Anthropology, and Mission in Trialogue*. Grand Rapids, MI: Zondervan, 1984.

Corbitt, J. Nathan. *The Sound of the Harvest: Music in Global Christianity*. Grand Rapids, MI: Baker, 1998.

Creswell, John W. *Qualitative Inquiry and Research Design: Choosing Among Five Approaches*. Thousand Oaks, CA: SAGE, 2007.

D'Andre, Roy. *The Development of Cognitive Anthropology*. Cambridge: Cambridge University Press, 1995.

Farhadian, Charles E., ed. *Christian Worship Worldwide: Expanding Horizons, Deepening Practices*. Grand Rapids, MI: Eerdmans, 2007.

Feld, Stephen. "Notes on World Beat." In *Music Grooves: Essays and Dialogues*, edited by Stephen and Charles Keil Feld, 238–46. Chicago: University of Chicago Press, 1994.

Fitzpatrick, Mary. *Mozambique*. Oakland, CA: Lonely Planet, 2007.

Flemming, Dean. *Contextualization in the New Testament: Patterns for Theology and Mission*. Downers Grove, IL: InterVarsity, 2005.

Fortier, Brad. "On the Road to a New Ethnography: Anthropology, Improvisation, and Performance." Interdisciplined (blog), January 12, 2011. https://bradfortier.com/2011/01/12/on-the-road-to-a-new-ethnography-anthropology-improvisation-and-performance/.

Fortunato, Frank, and Robin Harris. "The Crescendo of Local Arts in Orality." In *Orality Breakouts: Using Heart Language to Transform Hearts*, edited by Samuel Chiang et al., 113–18. Hong Kong: International Orality Network and Lausanne Committee for World Evangelism, 2010.

Frith, Simon. "Introduction, World Music, Politics and Social Change." In *Music and Society*, edited by Peter Martin and Simon Frith, 1–6. New York: Manchester University Press, 1989.

Geertz, Clifford. *The Interpretation of Cultures: Selected Essays*. New York: Basic Books, 1973.

Haleblian, Krikor. "The Problem of Contextualization." *Missiology* 10 (1983) 95–111.

Heifetz, Ronald A., and Marty Linsky. *Leadership On the Line: Staying Alive through the Dangers of Leading*. Boston: Harvard Business School Press, 2002.

Heifetz, Ronald A., Alexander Grashow, and Marty Linsky. *The Practice of Adaptive Leadership: Tools and Tactics for Changing Your Organization and the World*. Boston: Harvard Business School Press, 2009.

Hiebert, Paul G. *Anthropological Reflections on Missiological Issues*. Grand Rapids, MI: Baker, 1994.

Hiebert, Paul G., R. Daniel Shaw, and Tite Tiénou. *Understanding Folk Religion: A Christian Response to Popular Beliefs and Practices*. Grand Rapids, MI: Baker, 1999.

Higashi, Guy Scott Shigemi. "Musical Communitas: Gathering Around the Ukulele in Hawai'i and the Foursquare Church." D.Miss. diss., Fuller Theological Seminary, 2011.

Hustad, Donald. *Jubilate! Church Music in the Evangelical Tradition*. Carol Stream, IL: Hope Publishing, 1981.

Jones, A. M. *Studies in African Music*. London: Oxford University Press, 1959.
Kidula, Jean Ngoya. *Music in Kenyan Christianity: Logooli Religious Song*. Evanston: Indiana University Press, 2013.
King, Roberta R. *Music in the Life of the African Church*. Waco: Baylor University Press, 2008.
———. "Negotiating the Gospel Cross-Culturally: The Contributions of Intercultural Communication to Missiology." In *Paradigm Shifts in Christian Witness: Insights from Anthropology, Communication, and Spiritual Power*, edited by Charles E. Van Engen, Darrell Whiteman, and J. Dudley Woodberry, 66–76. Maryknoll, NY: Orbis, 2008.
———. *Pathways in Christian Music Communication: The Case of the Senufo of Côte d'Ivoire*. American Society of Missiology Monograph Series 3. Eugene, OR: Pickwick, 2009.
———. *A Time to Sing!* Nairobi, Kenya: Evangel Publishing, 1999.
———. "Toward a Discipline of Christian Ethnomusicology: A Missiological Paradigm." *Missiology* 32 (2004) 293–301.
Kisliuk, Michelle. "(Un)Doing Fieldwork." In *Shadows in the Field*, edited by Timothy J. Cooley and Gregory F. Barz, 183–205. New York: Oxford University Press, 1997.
Kraft, Charles H. *Anthropology for Christian Witness*. Maryknoll, NY: Orbis, 2000.
Leedy, Paul D., and Jeanne Ellis Ormrod. *Practical Research: Planning and Design*. 9th ed. Boston: Pearson Education, 2010.
Lingenfelter, Sherwood. *Agents of Transformation: A Guide for Effective Cross-Cultural Ministry*. Grand Rapids, MI: Baker, 1996.
———. *Leading Cross-Culturally: Covenant Relationships for Effective Christian Leadership*. Grand Rapids, MI: Baker, 2008.
———. *Transforming Culture: A Challenge for Christian Mission*. Grand Rapids, MI: Baker, 1998.
Lomax, A. "The Homogeneity of African-Afro-American Musical Style." In *Afro-American Anthropology: Contemporary Perspectives*, edited by N. E. Whitten Jr. and J. Szwed, 181–201. New York: Free Press, 1970.
Manuel, Peter. *Popular Music of the Non-Western World*. New York: Oxford University Press, 1988.
Masa, Bongaye Senza. "The Future of African Music." In *African Challenge*, edited by Kenneth Y. Best, 146–59. Nairobi, Kenya: Transafrica Publishers, 1975.
Massicame, Elias. "Ecumenism in Mozambique: In Search of Ecumenism That is Live-Giving and Healing." *Ecumenical Review* 53 (2001) 409–15.
McGann, Mary E. *Exploring Music as Worship and Theology*. Collegeville, MN: Liturgical, 2002.
McIntyre, Alice. *Participatory Action Research*. Thousand Oaks, CA: Sage, 2008 (Kindle ed.).
Meintjes, Louise. *Sound of Africa!* Durham: Duke University Press, 2003.
Merriam, Alan P. "African Music." In *Continuity and Change in African Cultures*, edited by W. R. Bascom and M. J. Herskovits, 49–86. Chicago: University of Chicago Press, 1959.
———. *The Anthropology of Music*. Evanston: Northwestern University Press, 1964.
Moreau, Scott. "Contextualization." In *The Changing Face of World Missions*, edited by Michael Pocock, Gailyn van Rheenen, and Douglas McConnell, 321–48. Grand Rapids, MI: Baker, 2005.

———. *Contextualization in World Missions*. Grand Rapids, MI: Kregel, 2012.

———. "Contextualization That is Comprehensive." *Missiology International Review* 34 (2006) 324–35.

Morgenthaler, Sally. *Worship Evangelism: Inviting Unbelievers Into the Presence of God*. Grand Rapids, MI: Zondervan, 1995.

"Multitree: A Digital Library of Language Relationships." Bloomington, IN: Department of Linguistics, The LINGUIST List, Indiana University, 2014. http://multitree.org.

Ndege, George O. *Culture and Customs of Mozambique*. Westport, CN: Greenwood, 2007.

Nettl, Bruno. *Eight Urban Musical Cultures: Tradition and Change*. Chicago: University of Illinois Press, 1978.

Newitt, Malyn. *A History of Mozambique*. Indianapolis: Indiana University Press, 1995.

Nhancalize, Domingos, et al. *Cançaó, Dança e Instrumentos de Música Tradicional nos Distritos de Búzi, Dondo e Marromeu, Província de Sofala*. Vol. 1. Beira, Mozambique: Imprensa Universitária, 2005.

Nketia, J. H. Kwabena. *The Music of Africa*. New York: Norton, 1974.

Parks, Sharon Daloz. *Leadership Can Be Taught: A Bold Approach for a Complex World*. Boston: Harvard Business School Press, 2005.

Piper, John. *Let the Nations Be Glad: The Supremacy of God in Missions*. Grand Rapids, MI: Baker, 1993.

Plueddemann, Jim. *Leading Across Cultures: Effective Ministry and Mission in the Global Church*. Downers Grove, IL: InterVarsity, 2009.

Rapport, Frances. "Summative Analysis: A Qualitative Method for Social Science and Health Research." *International Journal of Qualitative Methods* 9 (2010) 270.

Richardson, Don. *Eternity in Their Hearts*. Ventura, CA: Regal, 1981.

———. *Peace Child*. Ventura, CA: Regal, 1974.

Roberts, John Storm. *The Latin Tinge: The Impact of Latin American Music on the United States*. New York: Oxford University Press, 1979.

Schrag, Brian, and James R. Krabill, eds. *Creating Local Arts Together: A Manual to Help Communities Reach Their Kingdom Goals*. Pasadena, CA: William Carey, 2013.

Schreiter, Robert J. *Constructing Local Theologies*. Maryknoll, NY: Orbis, 1985.

Scott, Joyce. *Moving Into African Music*. Claremont, South Africa: PreText, 2009.

———. *Tuning In to a Different Song*. Fish Hoek, South Africa: University of Pretoria, 2000.

Seeger, Anthony. "Ethnography of Music." In *Ethnomusicology: An Introduction*, edited by H. Myers, 88–109. New York: Macmillian, 1992.

Shakespeare, William. *Hamlet*. London: Printed by Valentine Simmes for Nicholas Ling and Iohn Trundell, 1603.

Shelemay, Kay Kaufman. "Zema: A Concept of Sacred Music in Ethiopia." *The World of Music* 24 (1982) 52–67.

Sigler, Matthew. "Misplacing Charisma: Where Contemporary Christianity Lost Its Way." Seedbed, November 29, 2013. http://seedbed.com/feed/misplacing-charisma-contemporary-worship-lost-way/.

Smith, Donald K. *Creating Understanding: A Handbook for Christian Communication Across Cultural Landscapes*. Grand Rapids, MI: Zondervan, 1992.

Southern, Eileen. *The Music of Black Americans*. New York: Norton, 1971.

Spencer, Leon P. *Toward an African Church in Mozambique: Kamba Simango and the Protestant Community in Manica and Sofala, 1892-1945.* Lilongwe, Malawi: Mzuni Press, 2013.
Spradley, James P. *Participant Observation.* New York: Rinehart and Winston, 1980.
Stapleton, Chris, and Chris May. *African Rock: The Pop Music of a Continent.* New York: Dutton, 1989.
Steingo, G. "After Apartheid: Kwaito Music and the Aesthetics of Freedom." PhD diss., University of Pennsylvania, 2010.
Stone, Ruth M. *Let the Inside Be Sweet: The Interpretation of Music Event among the Kpelle of Liberia.* Bloomington: Indiana University Press, 1982.
Tan, Sooi Ling. "Transformative Worship Among the Salako in Sarawak, Malaysia." PhD diss., Fuller Theological Seminary, 2008.
Tarasti, Eero. *Signs of Music: A Guide to Musical Semiotics.* New York: Mouton de Gruyter, 2002.
Taylor, Timothy D. *Global Pop: World Music, World Markets.* New York: Routledge, 1997.
Titon, Jeff Todd, ed. *Worlds of Music: An Introduction to the Music of the World's Peoples.* Belmont, CA: Schrimer, 2009.
Tracey, Hugh. *Chopi Musicians: Their Music, Poetry, and Instruments.* London: Oxford University Press, 1948.
Turino, Thomas. *Music as Social Life: The Politics of Participation.* Chicago: University of Chicago Press, 2008.
———. *Nationalists, Cosmopolitans, and Popular Music in Zimbabwe.* Chicago: University of Chicago Press, 2000.
———. "Signs of Imagination, Identity, and Experience: A Peircian Semiotic Theory for Music." *Ethnomusicology* 43 (1999) 221–55.
Turner, Victor. *Dramas, Fields and Metaphors.* Ithaca: Cornell University Press, 1974.
Wachsmann, K. P. "Human Migration and African Harps." *Journal of the International Folk Music Council* 16 (1964) 84–88.
Walls, Andrew F. "The Gospel As the Prisoner and Liberator of Culture." *Missionalia* 10 (1982) 93–105.
———. *The Missionary Movement in Christian History: Studies in the Transmission of Faith.* Maryknoll, NY: Orbis, 1996.
Waterman, Christopher. "Africa." In *Ethnomusicology: Historical and Regional Studies,* edited by Helen Myers, 240–60. New York: Norton, 1993.
———. *Juju: A Social History and Ethnography of an African Popular Music.* Chicago: University of Chicago Press, 1990.
———. "The Uneven Development of Africanist Ethnomusicology: Three Issues and a Critique." In *Comparative Musicology and Anthropology of Music: Essays on the History of Ethnomusicology,* edited by Bruno Nettle and Philip V. Bohlman, 169–86. Chicago: University of Chicago Press, 1991.
Webber, Robert. *Signs of Wonder: The Phenomenon of Convergence in Modern Liturgical and Charismatic Churches.* Nashville: Abbott Martyn, 1992.
Witvliet, John. "Teaching Worship as a Christian Practice." In *For Life Abundant: Practical Theology, Theological Education, and Christian Ministry,* edited by Dorothy C. Bass and Craig Dykstra, 117–49. Grand Rapids, MI: Eerdmans, 2008.
Yin, Robert K. *Case Study Research: Design and Methods.* Thousand Oaks, CA: SAGE, 1994.

www.ingramcontent.com/pod-product-compliance
Lightning Source LLC
Chambersburg PA
CBHW051742230426
43670CB00012B/2128